WITH ALL OUR
HEART AND MIND

WITH ALL OUR HEART AND MIND

The Spiritual Works of Mercy in a Psychological Age

Sidney Callahan

Crossroad • New York

1988

The Crossroad Publishing Company
370 Lexington Avenue, New York, N.Y. 10017

Printed in the United States of America

Library of Congress Cataloging-in-Publication Data

Callahan, Sidney Cornelia.
  With all our heart and mind : the spiritual works of mercy in a
psychological age / Sidney Callahan.
      p.   cm.
  ISBN 0-8245-0843-2
  1. Spiritual works of mercy.   2. Spiritual life—Catholic authors.
I. Title.
BV4647.M4C34   1988
241—dc19   87-34574
                                                        CIP

*I gratefully dedicate this book
to my aunt, Olive Sharrett de Shazo,
whose love and spiritual witness has deeply affected my life.*

Contents

INTRODUCTION

WHY RECONSIDER THE SPIRITUAL WORKS OF MERCY?

The corporal and spiritual works of mercy have long been enumerated in Church tradition in sets of seven each. The corporal works of mercy are:

> To feed the hungry
> To give drink to the thirsty
> To clothe the naked
> To visit those in prison
> To shelter the homeless
> To bury the dead.
> To give hospitality to the stranger.

The spiritual works of mercy are:

> To admonish the sinner
> To instruct the ignorant
> To counsel the doubtful
> To comfort the sorrowful
> To bear wrongs patiently
> To forgive all injuries
> To pray for the living and the dead.

When asked to recall these lists, individuals can remember some of the first, but fail to remember the second. I think the selective forgetting of the spiritual works of mercy has an explanation. For centuries the corporal works of mercy have remained much the same, but the spiritual works of mercy must be reinterpreted and reappropriated as a culture changes. Since there has been no recent attention given to renewing our understanding of the spiritual works of mercy, they have faded from the collective consciousness. By contrast, the physical needs of human beings remain constant. Whatever the time or place, the human body does not change its requirements for food, drink, shelter, nursing, succor, and a final resting place. We can see a clear need, and we know what the Christian response should be, whether in a Calcutta slum, an Ethiopian refugee camp, or on the Upper East Side of Manhattan.

Our vision is less clear, however, when we confront "spiritual" needs requiring "spiritual action." With changes in our psychological, social, and theological understanding of human persons, neither the need nor the appropriate response is obvious. How exactly in the present context of my life do I go about admonishing sinners or counseling the doubtful? And surely it is necessary to reinterpret the meaning of bearing wrongs patiently in the light of liberation theology, assertiveness training, and the ongoing struggles for human rights. Our thought patterns and spiritual needs in late-twentieth-century America do not differ totally from those of earlier Christians (else the spiritual classics would not endure), but our spiritual concerns are different enough to warrant a serious reconsideration of the place of the spiritual works of mercy in our common Christian life.

I can remember my frustration when as a young enthusiast I would devour one traditional spiritual classic or saint's biography after another, only to remain unsatisfied in my search for the perfect model for my spiritual life. Like Augustine, I took and read the book, and the next book, and the next, without finding a solution to my problem. In every work I would find wonderful insights, but no ready-made pattern of life to follow. It took years before the truth finally broke through: Sidney, you are not going to find your perfect model because no one before you has lived with the changing cultural conditions you are experiencing. Face it: American Christians have to be creative to cope with this chaotic time of medical, technological, and social revolution.

With hindsight, I can see that the blueprints for the spiritual life inherited from the past were unsuitable for those of us living with new American class structures, gender roles, sexual expectations, and educational opportunities. Even in the secular domain, women were bereft of role models. Like many other middle-class educated women married to professional men, I aspired to have children and a career. Since I wanted six children I was prepared to wait a decade or so before leaving the house, but I would still study and write at home. Our generation was merging social roles previously kept separate: while thoroughly engrossed in the psychological and physical demands of family life, without servants or social support, we were also immersed in professional work. The secular pluralistic society in which we moved was indifferent, if not downright hostile, to family and spiritual concerns, and the Church was not much more understanding of the dilemmas faced by the educated laity.

Certainly, Christians in past eras managed to live spiritual lives in intensely worldly settings (as in the court of Louis XIV, for example), but never before had individuals faced so many different levels of complicated demands with so little leisure or social support. In one day I might be washing diapers and cleaning the bathroom, struggling through a philosophy text for a writing assignment, rushing to a child's school function, and from there home to prepare a dinner party for my husband's colleagues. During the unceasing night-and-day duty of the early childbearing years, even the Trappists' routine seemed comparatively self-indulgent. When children have grown up, family demands recede somewhat, but professional and volunteer commitments increase. Most traditional spir-

itual writers probably would not have been able to compre-
hend American lives crammed with work, study, and activity,
lives that at the same time are filled to the brim with marriage, childbearing, child rearing, and the perpetual roller
coaster (or should I say continuing soap opera?) of family life
in turbulent times.

Unfortunately, much of today's writing on living the spiritual life seems equally unsatisfying. Some books seem too
woolly with high-flown rhetoric, others too concrete and sim-
plistic. Alas, it may also be the case that some of today's
spiritual writers are writing for people who are much more
advanced than the majority of us, who still struggle on the
bottom rung of the spiritual ladder. But perhaps the most
serious problem is the failure to achieve a synthesis of psychological knowledge with spiritual truths. Today we live in a
culture so suffused with psychology that we need psychologically astute pathfinders through the therapeutic thickets of
spiritual and psychological literature. A new in-depth integration is needed: too often the psychological self-help books
scant spirituality while many spiritual works are not psychologically sophisticated enough. Even the spiritual writers who
attempt to incorporate psychology often founder. It will not do
for Christians to baptize popular psychology (aptly termed
psychobabble), nor should they canonize one or another psychological theorist (such as Jung.) As I attempt to reconsider
the spiritual works of mercy, I shall employ all the psychological astuteness I can muster as both psychologist and Christian.

I can note at once that today the Church probably would
not choose to divide the works of mercy into separate corporal
and spiritual compartments. This division reflects a gnostic
view of the human being in which the spirit is like a ghost in
the machine of the body. Advances in both our theological
thinking and vast psychological and medical evidence now
convince us that the mind and body are fused in a unitary

whole. Illness can affect the mind; thinking and emotions can affect the body. The interaction is two-way and immensely complex. Psychosomatic medicine has been vindicated, and is now reborn as behavioral medicine and health psychology. We are our bodies, our bodies are our selves.

But at the same time we are also more than our bodies. As a person I can view the aging or illness of that aspect of me that is my body, and see "it" as separate from some essence of "me." An adult human being exists with a hierarchy of operations: my mind, emotions, and will are in some sense more important to me than my body's function. Who does not fear psychosis, Alzheimer's Disease, or other destroyers of the self far more than blindness or some physical handicap? We also know that our bodies can enjoy the best of health and be exercised into perfect fitness, and yet we are still miserable or in despair. The young, the healthy, the beautiful, the well-nourished, and the affluent regularly kill themselves. They throw their perfectly maintained bodies out of high windows. It is not enough to have corporal needs fulfilled.

The traditional division of corporal and spiritual works of mercy makes sense when it is seen rather as a difference in the focus of attention and emphasis. Physician and psychologist are different if overlapping professions. We must always take into account the spirit and dignity of the unique person when we perform the corporal works of mercy. But it is also the case that spiritual needs may exist in those who do not require physical care; at most one might offer cups of tea, or meals, or walks, or busying tasks, or comfortable seats before the fire, or even physical affection, along with comfort, counsel, or confrontation. In such cases the spiritual need and our spiritual response are the important thing.

WHAT COUNTS AS "SPIRIT" OR "SPIRITUAL?"

How are we going to use the word *spirit*, as in a spiritual work or spiritual need? Confusion arises over these terms because we have not yet found a new Christian synthesis integrating the modern psychologies and theological under-standings of the human person. Ever since the admirable Thomistic system fell into disuse, Christians (along with everyone else) have had no compelling theory of personality. Today the fields of psychiatry and psychology study the mind and the emotions, but our psychology of personality still exists at a very primitive level, far below the developed consensus of other scientific disciplines. There is no dominant theory or paradigm to which all investigators give assent. Behaviorists, sociobiologists, neo-Freudians, developmentalists, cognitive psychologists, humanistic existentialists, and various others are still battling over the territory. No theory has decisively triumphed and most contain enough truth to be supported by some concrete evidence. At the same time within theology there exist new questions about the definitions and interrela-tionships of person, body, self, mind, soul, spirit, and Holy Spirit. Pulling together a synthesis of two bodies of thought in turbulent transition is not an easy task. Therefore when I offer my tentative definition of spirit within a Christian theory of personality, it is offered as a first step toward the new syn-thesis we badly need, even to order our practical everyday actions.

I interpret the spirit of a person to mean the personal conscious activity that emerges beyond bodily functioning and beyond unconscious determining forces of the past and present environment. Since theologically we know that grace works through nature, the human spirit can be seen as that same activating force of reason, emotion, will, and disposi-tions which some psychologists and philosophers call the self or person. The more traditional concept of the soul includes the self or spirit but is more inclusive. In order to avoid the many theological controversies over the nature of the soul, I think the soul can best be thought of as referring to the whole existing human being's life as known to God. The individual human spirit or person or self seems the dimension of the soul psychologically knowable to ourselves and others. Thus the *spirit* involved in the needs and works of the spiritual works of mercy is that active, unique, self-conscious capacity for personal consciousness in human persons. A spiritual need is a need of a unique individual person, and a spiritual work is a personal conscious act of an individual self. These spiritual phenomena are person-to-person interactions from one self-conscious self to another.

My definition of *spirit* is that part of the human personality accessible to conscious awareness or available to self-consciousness. But to identify the human spirit with the conscious self does not deny the existence of other dimensions or systems within the complex human organism. I think that the human spirit or conscious self emerges from and interrelates constantly with the functioning of the body, with the functioning of the unconscious and preconscious dimensions of the personality, and, most mysteriously of all, with the operations of the indwelling divine presence. Thus, many things going on within us exist beyond conscious awareness. The brain regulates the body in miraculous feats of order, growth, healing, and homeostasis.

Clearly, the mind functions in part unconsciously (as when we are unconscious, asleep, or amnesiac), but the functions and limits of the unconscious mind are a matter of dispute among psychologists. The status of dreams, for example, is questioned. Sleep researchers tell us that sleep and dreams come in different stages and varieties, so all claims about dreams have some validity. Some dreams may be, as Freud and Jung insisted, meaningful messages from the unconscious; other dreams, as some psychologists have recently proposed, may simply result from the mind discharging the residue of mental computer programs. Dreams in other states of sleep may be intrusions of bits of everyday reality. Whatever their exact status, these functions of the human person are not the self-conscious, aware, awake acts of what I am calling the self or spirit involved in spiritual works.

Between fully aware self-consciousness and completely opaque unconscious operations there are other graduated degrees of consciousness, some right on the edge of full awareness and others almost merged with the unconsciousness of sleep. These in-between modes of human activity, such as occur in daydreaming and under hypnosis, are intensely fascinating and present puzzling questions: Can we control these states? Are we responsible for them? Are these aspects of the self or spirit? It seems clear that these preconscious, or not-quite-conscious human operations include much of the personal temperament, conceptual style, and habits that constitute personality. As human beings we possess personal characteristics that are unique, individual, automatic, habitual, and mostly outside of our full personal awareness. Other people can see these things in us, but we habitually fail to see them in ourselves (just as we rarely confront the way our body looks from behind).

Important preconscious dimensions of personality seem stored in an individual's long-term memory. Like habits and conditioned responses, our memories are only partly under conscious control. Psychologists are studying how personal memories get encoded and stored, how memories are retrieved, and how memory influences perception and thinking. It now seems evident that there is an ongoing preconscious filtering or selection process that accounts for the perceptions and thoughts that we experience as effortlessly 'coming to mind.' But who or what selects and with what criteria? Some fascinating new theories even posit a 'hidden observer' within, monitoring information flow beyond self-consciousness. With conscious efforts we can bring things to mind or at least start searching in memory for something we sense we know. If we start trying to remember and fail, sometime later what we were looking for may suddenly come to us. All these are mysterious operations somewhere between full voluntary conscious activity and unconsciousness.

It also seems clear that some information we might easily notice, know, or remember, is curiously forgotten, ignored, or overlooked. These selective omissions and distortions seem to serve defensive purposes of different sorts. Psychoanalysis has found that human beings avoid pain or seek pleasure through such preconscious selective maneuvers of the mind. Should these almost-out-of-awareness activities count as actions of the self or spirit? They are surely part of the personality but while they remain out of consciousness I don't think they should be included as activities of the self or spirit. Only when something that has been automatic, preconscious, or unconscious comes into awareness and becomes accessible to and is appropriated by the conscious self, does it truly become personal, truly part of my self.

Although I am identifiably the same individual when I am drugged or dreaming or in a state of shock, I cannot be said to be fully my self. My dreams or preconscious defenses may be mainly automatic products of my personality, just as my physical symptoms may be products of my body's unconscious regulating system. But while some things are out of my direct control, I can still be indirectly responsible for much of my automatic personal functioning. If I know that alcohol intoxicates me and makes me not my self, I am responsible if I drink too much. If I am suffering from a disease such as epilepsy or diabetes that can be controlled by taking my medication and I don't do it, I am indirectly responsible for my state when I become impaired. We are also responsible for many of our emotional states, as we shall see in future chapters. The old strategy of avoiding sin by avoiding the occasions of sin is quite pertinent here.

The experience of being a self or spirit only partially in control of one's person is a universal one and has been a perennial intellectual problem for reflective thinkers. Aristotle spoke of *akrasia*, or "weakness of will" and Saint Paul voiced the common human condition when he cried out "that which I would do, I do not; and that which I would not, I do." Paul's description of the spirit warring against the flesh may also refer to one's conscious self in relation to one's recalcitrant, more unconsciously determined personality characteristics. The Gospel's references to transformation, sanctification, liberation, and "putting on the new man," can be interpreted as referring to the process by which the conscious self or spirit becomes more and more the owner and self-regulator of the whole person. The ultimate hope seems to be that this process of transformation can extend to the human body resurrected after death. Christians have always believed this liberation and transformation of the human being can only be accomplished through the redemptive power of Christ living and acting within the person. The process depends upon the self or spirit's voluntary opening to God's power through faith, hope, and love, through prayer, worship, and good works. The promise of the Gospel is that God will be found within the human being, as well as without.

THE SPIRIT AND THE HOLY SPIRIT

The final challenge in attempts to define the spirit, or self, is relating the human spirit to the indwelling Trinity promised by Christ. We believe that God is immanent in Creation as well as transcendently beyond it. But we don't know exactly how the Creator has separated an independent creation and human creatures while at the same time grounding their existence in divine love and power. It is a mystery of simultaneous transcendence and immanence that we can only dimly understand and experience. The belief of Christians has been that God, Christ, and the Holy Spirit reside within us and in them we move and live and have our being. But at the same time, the divine Spirit is separate from the individual human spirit and self; we experience ourselves as free, with independent responses.

We are aware that our movements to open ourselves to God come from some prior divine invitation and initiative of love, but as free spirits we are able to respond in different ways. I can accept, ignore, or refuse the invitation. The mystery is that when I act in a good way I am somehow completely free and yet moved and strengthened by God's loving power. It's like riding on a passenger conveyer at an airport: you can either stand still and be carried, or walk along on the miraculously flowing path. God's grace is similar: you can move ahead through your own individually willed actions but the conveyor so propels you onward that you feel you are truly flying forward to your destination in a cooperative venture. It's also appropriate to the analogy to remember that persons who are too burdened with luggage can rest a while and still be carried along. And yes, there are travelers who scorn the conveyor and choose the unassisted hard way; these people are still better off than the perverse souls who insist on fighting their way backward against the flow of assistance.

Once a person has experienced the divine assistance within, it is possible to repeatedly seek the Spirit's aid. The ordinary operation of human conscience is an example of an inner dialogue that is assisted by the Holy Spirit within the personality. Conscience has even been identified as the light of the Holy Spirit within each person. The image of the light within or inner light has been used to describe these experiences of divine immanence. Other examples of turning one's self over to God's grace and power are also practiced in and out of Christianity. I think that many of the self-help movements, such as Alcoholics Anonymous, are examples of the self's opening the personality to the indwelling Spirit's influence. (We shall discuss this in more detail in later chapters.) Just as one can indirectly open oneself to intoxicating or evil influences so one can open oneself to the work of the Holy Spirit within. The self or spirit is gradually changed by repeated acts of attention and focused energies, whether to good or evil. God's good work of inner psychological transformation has been called by various names: grace, the infusion of virtues, sanctification. We may not completely understand it, but we do experience it.

HOW DOES THE HUMAN SPIRIT DEVELOP?

While the human spirit or self is a separate and individual consciousness, no individual human being can come into existence or come to God alone. Perhaps archangels are truly self-sufficient spirits but human beings are firmly embedded in a collective existence. The wonderfully unique individual self that we possess is a gift of our genetic inheritance and social experience. There is no self-made man or woman. The birth of the self is a gradual process built up from genetic predispositions and capacities interacting with the interpersonal experiences of infancy. Full self-consciousness emerges from many prior experiences of infancy and childhood. Each of us was already a unique personality at our first birthday party but we do not start being the continuous conscious selves we are as adults until much later. God may call us into being at the moment of conception and knows us from our mother's womb, but we do not self-consciously know ourselves until much later.

The social creation of the conscious self grows out of the dialogue of the infant with the world and other persons. The emotional dialogue of sense and feeling may be the most basic way we interact with others in our first experiences. The perceptual interchange of smell, touch, sound, gaze, warmth, feeding, and bathing produces the bonding and attachment from which a conscious self emerges. The mutual gaze of infant and caretaker is particularly significant and provides the model for romantic love and the image of the blissful beatific vision. Being looked at, attended to, cared for, played with, and talked to creates the self that is born from the mutual human exchange. The infant is genetically programmed for this participation with caretakers. Without it an infant will waste away or die. The infant is selectively attuned to faces and emotional exchanges and, most important, is innately prepared to learn language. Whatever language group the infant is born into, he or she will rhythmically respond to it and begin to absorb its rules, rhythms, and vocabulary long before being able to speak.

With the coming of the word and the gradual mastery of language, the self takes a gigantic leap into humanhood. The rush into language is nearly miraculous; the mind's abilities to process experience then increases geometrically, along with the growth of self-consciousness. When a small child first speaks the words *me* and *I*, the personality has given birth to the self-conscious self. The continuity of our innate inner emotional experiences combined with the human dialogue creates the spirit and self that can reflect upon itself as an "I." Descartes should have said, "I think, I feel, I know others, therefore I am." The human spirit is a gift we receive from the care and communication of our caretakers. Human caretakers treat the baby as though it were a self, through play and talk and care, and through this expectant interchange they create the self in response. When we affirm that God first loved us and called us into the life of grace, we are describing a process similar to the initial human attention and attachments which create the self. Each human person is partially created through the spiritual and corporal works of mercy of their parents and other members of their community.

The human motivation engendering the process of bringing a self into existence is natural, innate love. Defining love in its purely natural sense of attachment, bonding, and attentive care is not difficult. Emotions have now been rehabilitated and newly recognized in social science. Psychologists now theorize that the human species has survived because of its capacities for emotions that facilitate adaptation and survival. The innate primary emotional building blocks of the human species are found everywhere and in every culture; they are listed as interest-excitement, joy-ecstasy, sorrow-sadness, anger-rage, shame-humiliation, contempt-disgust, and remorse-guilt. Love is a primary fusion of interest and joy which produces bonding attachment. The emotions motivate human survival and the creation of culture, and the positive emotion of love produces the bonds that keep the nurturing family and community cohesively cooperating. Through evolutionary selection human beings come into the world innately prepared to love and be loved; adults in their turn are predisposed to love and care for infants. The older pessimistic psychoanalytic views describing human nature as selfish and aggressive have been complemented with discoveries of innate tendencies toward empathy, sympathy, altruism, and love.

Christian definitions of love, or *agape*, or charity are firmly based upon natural human predispositions selected by evolutionary forces. But innate good traits are not the whole inheritance. Aggression, selfishness, even self-deception are also innately a part of human nature. (In terms of old theological disputes, the best psychological estimate of our human nature seems to be that we are wounded but not depraved.)

WHAT IS THE PLACE OF THE SPIRITUAL WORKS OF MERCY IN OUR LIFE TOGETHER?

We belong to a social species whose members depend upon human bonds and attachments to survive and flourish. Humans must love and care for each other but are imperfectly prepared to do so. Because human weaknesses and sin are always present, and because of the disordered world in which we find ourselves, every human being needs others. Christians affirm that our human response to life should be to love God with our whole heart and mind, and our neighbor as our self. Theologians now make it clear that love of God and love of neighbor are essentially one and the same, for God is in each of His creatures as well as transcendently beyond all imagining. In Scripture Christ tells us that what we do for the least of our fellow human beings we do for him. From these Gospel injunctions to love and work toward God's kingdom, the Church articulated the traditional teachings on the works of mercy.

The works of mercy are a Christian's response to God's love; they are love in action. In grateful imitation of God's love and mercy to us, Christians attempt to "be merciful as your Father in heaven is merciful." Of course there is a vast difference in what humans can do compared to God's love and power, but we are still called to do what we can. As wounded imperfect persons we do not do works of mercy as though we possess all good things in abundance and dispense them at will. A Lady Bountiful distributing turkeys, baskets of cheer, and instruction is the wrong image. A spiritual or personal psychological work of mercy is not simply a matter of giving things that we have to those without. It must be a very different process. Central to understanding this process is a grasp of the idea that thoughts, prayers, emotions, speech, or goodwill are not really "things" but are essentially personal actions. Acts directed to other self-conscious persons are enacted in a dynamic interrelationship that affects us as we act. In consciousness-to-consciousness communication we change as we reach out to one another. Understanding this mutuality I can quite humbly undertake things that would be inappropriate and arrogant if viewed as a one-way directive or gift from a superior to an inferior.

Fortunately, modern psychologists have come up with an old but new-sounding concept of "the wounded healer." Who can better understand and help another person than one who has suffered the same weakness or can empathetically experience it. In modern forms of personal mediation, those who have recovered from an addiction, those who have been in prison, and those who have been through other crises are acknowledged as those most able to help the similarly afflicted: "I can understand you, I have been there." The incarnational principle that those who have lived through a situation can best help others justifies the Christian efforts to offer help. Every Christian conscious of sin, personal suffering, and the need to be healed can try to meet another's need.

The spiritual or psychological works of mercy are necessary because we have all experienced suffering and the brokenness of life to a certain degree. Who has not sinned, doubted, been ignorant, or hurt? We have all been there, and can respond in love to our fellow beings when they suffer or lose their way. As wounded healers we can reach out to others with humility whatever our stage of spiritual development. Fortunately, we do not have to have reached the illuminated way, or have experienced mystical heights to engage in these ordinary enterprises of daily life among ordinary people. All of us can reconsider and reflect on what these spiritual or self-giving efforts will mean today. And of course there will be different times in our lives when certain works of mercy or ways of loving are more appropriate than others.

Life as we lead it, whether stumbling along or purposefully marching to meet goals, has a way of presenting us with unexpected challenges. Fervent youth may champ at the bit seeking heroic challenge and sacrifices. Older pilgrims know that what turns up will be hard enough. The great Saint Teresa had youthful visions of herself going off to martyrdom among the Moors, but she found dealing with the pettiness and inertia of the people at home enough of a challenge. My own observation has been that everyone, regardless of vocation or goals, eventually experiences a well-rounded spiritual curriculum. Nuns or married women, priests or fathers of families, professionals or peasants, every temperament and intellect seems to need and to receive specifically tailored tutoring to learn to love God and neighbor. These varied experiences cannot all happen at the same time, of course, so persons look as though they are on much more distinct ventures than may really be the case. When we see someone whose life seems spiritually easy, so smoothly flowing, so untroubled by temptation or struggle, I think that we should remember that every life is lived in stages over time. We do not know what has already been struggled with or what may yet come, and our outsider's perspective is very different from a person's inner experience. The same can also be true of lives that outwardly seem unbearably crushed by misfortune, although we should not for this reason feel indifferent or apathetic toward the suffering of others.

God is definitely a God of surprises. New experiences and challenges, both joyful and excruciating, can occur in even the most routine life. In my experience, those who seek God are never bored or becalmed for long. Most of us will never reach those spiritual depths where the saints suffered extended dark nights of the soul. But the testimony seems to be that, even for them, periods of dryness finally pass and give way to new times of growth. Periods of jogging along uneventfully seem relatively brief. Just as we think we have mastered some stage or challenge in life, it changes. Unexpected joys may suddenly come: C. S. Lewis entitled his autobiography *Surprised by Joy*, and he was wise to do so; long after he wrote his book he found new love and a late marriage with a woman named Joy. But it is also true that we can be caught off guard by some particular suffering we could not imagine ever having to confront. After his unexpected idyllic marriage, C. S. Lewis had to suffer the early death of his wife, with all the agonies he could hardly have foreseen in his days as a self-sufficient Oxford don

Like Lewis and everyone else, I too have experienced more joyful things in life than I could ever have dreamed were coming. And like others, I have also experienced suffering and traumas that were total shocks from out of the blue: the sudden death of a parent, a child, an emergency operation, a devastating betrayal of love. In the human condition a person can be catapulted from a totally joyful condition in which all is happiness to the deepest grief, sorrow, and anxiety. In my life unexpected sufferings and crises produced a complete reliance upon God and responsive spiritual acts of mercy on the part of my friends. God rescues us out of the depths of misery and friends offer support. Spiritual assistance is less dramatic but still present in the more slowly developing problems of life that produce chronic suffering: the alienation of a child, problems with alcoholism or disease, struggles with work, or financial problems.

While joys and grace abound, life is also hard. We all need to help and be helped as we struggle on. The great novelist Henry James has his characters ask their friends in moments of stress, "Will you see me through?"—through illness, betrayal, or the task of overcoming evil. So, too, all of us who attempt to lead a Christian life need others to see us through. The spiritual works of mercy are ways that we do this for one another. All such psychological efforts require energy. God makes such expenditures of energy possible, and occasionally even easy to do, but often we have to work against our natural inertia and laziness. It is so much easier not to get involved; the slang expression "Who needs it?" sums up our natural resistance to becoming enmeshed with others when we would just as soon retreat.

Listening to the Church's demand for love and works of mercy spurs us on. Within the tradition of the Church the range of the corporal and spiritual works of mercy serves as a corrective to our penchant for designing a narrower Christian life. Just as the unexpected joys, opportunities, and sufferings that come our way push us in undreamed-of directions, so the breadth of the works of mercy challenges us to expand and expend ourselves. All of these different ways of expressing charity will challenge us at different times and in different situations. Naturally, some actions will be more difficult for us than others; the great struggle in the self's interaction with others is getting things into balance and proportion.

In fact, if one type of action is too easy for us we might be suspicious of our motivation. Am I always, for example, too eager to admonish the sinner, or too ready to weep with the bereaved? Or is it always easier for me to bear wrongs patiently than risk conflict by admonishing the sinner? In God, justice and mercy are joined, but we find it difficult to discern ways to practice both. None of the spiritual acts of mercy come with ready-made patterns to follow.

HOW THIS BOOK IS ORGANIZED

This book contains seven chapters, one for each of the traditional spiritual works of mercy. The traditional order in which they are given reveals to my mind an ascending scale of spiritual and psychological difficulty. It is much easier to admonish sinners or instruct the ignorant than to forgive injuries or pray for others. Is this an intentional ordering of the list, or one of those ways in which Church communal tradition embodies implicit truths that have never been articulated? Piaget, the great developmental psychologist, recognizes a law of human development that applies as well to the Church's development over the centuries of its life. Piaget observed that children can actually perform intelligent problem solving before they are able to articulate what they are doing. In fact their verbal descriptions of what they are doing is couched in the immature inaccurate language they are about to outgrow. They can do it, they just can't fully articulate what they know. Becoming psychologically self-conscious, or growing in spirit and truth, takes time, whether the development is taking place in a person or the Church. Christians are gradually coming to understand what has been done for us in the Creation and The Redemption, and slowly growing in the ability to articulate our communal response. Reflecting upon our traditions and present experience is one way we progress in understanding.

I will treat each of the traditional spiritual works of mercy and reflect upon them in different ways. But the major focus of my attention will not be on the past, but on what these psychological actions of the self or spirit mean for us as persons living today in our pluralistic, complicated world.

Intellectually, our time is a period of ferment, rightly labeled I think, as the beginning of the postmodern world. Many secular idols are crashing down around us. In the past Christians have flourished when an old order gave way. The barbarians at the gates never meant the end, but only a new opportunity. I think this is also a propitious time for the development of Christianity and the forging of a new intellectual syntheses more open to the Spirit of Truth. My modest effort is to rethink the spiritual works of mercy from a psychological perspective.

1

TO ADMONISH THE SINNER

If your brother does something wrong, go and have it out with him alone, between your two selves. If he listens to you, you have won back your brother. (Matthew 18:15)

In wisdom made perfect, instruct and admonish one another. (Colossians 3:16)

A spiritual work of mercy in these psychologically knowledgeable times can be thought of as a conscious effort to enact God's love and imitate God's mercy in the inner life of thought and feeling. Like all mercy it is a form of love in action, a way of meeting human need. The spiritual works of mercy are psychological acts which arise from our innermost personal selves and are directed to another's innermost personal needs of heart and mind. They are unique person-to-person transactions—demanding full attention, mindfulness of self, and consciousness of others as unique selves.

ADMONISHING THE SINNER

What does psychologically supportive love and mercy have to do with "admonishing the sinner"? To admonish the sinner is given first place in the traditional list of the seven spiritual works of mercy, but to our modern ears it is repellent, inducing images of Savonarola thundering damnation, or fundamentalist preachers hurling invective and threats of hellfire. In the present age of tolerance, we can't help but wonder whether we have the right to judge or admonish another.

Those committed to Christian charity wonder whether admonishing sinners is compatible with love: we are told to refrain from judging others. The concept of sin also presents some difficulty for us. Am I even sure that there really *are* sinners out there? And if there are, how do I know who they are, or go about admonishing them?

On reflection perhaps the question of whether sinners exist or not, is the easiest question to settle. Are there sinners? Yes. After all, I know of at least one sinner, namely, myself. Even though I try not to, I sin. This rather compelling firsthand evidence of personal sin leads to the obvious generalization: I am not alone in my sinning. Unfortunately it is clear that I sin, you sin, he, she, and we sin. While it is doubtful that many of us engage in serious mortal sins, we do sin often.

THE FACT OF SIN

The kind of sins most of us commit seem not to be of the dread mortal kind; they are not fully premeditated, completely calculated, free and final rejections of God's goodness and truth in a serious matter. If we are to believe the more optimistic theologians, there may be relatively few mortal sinners among us. From a psychological perspective, many of the gruesome acts we read about in the newspapers can hardly be considered freely committed mortal sins. These crimes seem much too crazy, too much like mental illness, brain seizures, or poisoned toxic states in which persons lose all voluntary control. Perhaps individuals are responsible for getting into such out-of-control states by not seeking help, not taking medication, not abstaining from drugs, not resisting selfish habits of immediate gratification; but once people have become possessed, drugged, or crazed, they can hardly be free enough to consciously and voluntarily sin with full knowledge of what they are doing. They perpetuate evil, commit crimes, and cause untold harm, but they do not seem to be committing mortal sins.

More normal people may also rarely commit mortal sins. It seems sensible to hold that only at the moment of death when one confronts God directly, *for sure*, only at that moment of clarity could one ever understand enough, or be free enough, to irrevocably reject God's grace. In everyday life, many persons may never operate freely enough to be as reprehensible as they appear. The newest psychological research on the mind seems to confirm the existence of powerful unconscious and preconscious automatic determinants of our thought and behavior. So much filtering goes on outside awareness in our ordinary processing of information, that our freedom seems rather more limited than classical theories of freedom have supposed.

Yes, we *can* make free conscious choices, but our personality characteristics interacting with our inherited neurochemistry gradually take on a life of their own. As many before and after Saint Paul have testified, we do evil things we have not consciously willed to do. On the other hand it is also the case that our automatic reactive personalities can be habitually virtuous, so that some persons find it almost impossible to do wrong. For most of us, unfortunately, our inertia more often produces automatic evil acts and strong resistances to changes for the better. Habitual weaknesses can produce a blindness to self and lack of self-control, which, like the psychotic's craziness, may keep many from having enough freedom to truly commit mortal sins. In a sense it is true that only highly controlled, integrated characters can be strong enough for great sins. The anxiety that saints display over their sins may reflect the accurate perception that they are more capable of more serious sins than the rest of us. Greater self-discipline, an achieved self-mastery combined with a greater knowledge of good and evil than most, puts a person at greater risk of freely sinning.

Usually, sin enters ordinary lives through a passive consent to self-deception and other defensive mental moves meant to avoid the voice of conscience. Sin seems only partially premeditated, and so remains in the venial category. When faced with a temptation, we give in by quickly brushing aside or suppressing conscious misgivings; by these moves we allow ourselves to do what we want to do, when we want to do it. I rush to give my destructive bit of gossip, or to deliver my scathing sarcasm to an opponent. We also become quite adept at quickly resisting demands for love or justice which move us; after a disturbed minute or two, we manage to resubmerge ourselves in comfort, and inert laziness. I turn away and harden my heart against the appeal for my time, or money, or action. Our predisposition to avoid pain and seek pleasure and ease helps us to avoid penetrating self-confrontation; we collude with ourselves in bursts of bad faith and don't want to attend to what we're really doing—or really feeling. Camus said that the good person is the one who has the fewest lapses of attention. Letting our attention selectively lapse is the essence of self-deception.

THE SINFUL SELF

At times, we become more actively ensnared in overt sin and nurse anger, bitterness, and envy; we cleverly and subtly seek revenge or another's harm, or try to mar another's happiness or advancement. Once we give in to sin, sin quickly escalates by way of the defensive efforts we must take to suppress guilt, remorse, or repentance. We start to lie and to blame others rather than face the shame of our own wrong-doing. Well-intentioned, fairly normal people can get caught in obsessions or addictions or illusions they absolutely refuse to give up, despite their recognition that what they are doing is both morally wrong and self-destructive. Guilt, shame, and fear fuse with self-loathing, goading individuals on to further sin; they must continue in order to resist the pressure to concede the immorality of their actions. Out of pride they refuse fully to admit their fault.

Like Lucifer, humans can also cry, *"Non serviam"* (I "will not serve," or give in to God, love, truth, or reality). I *will* keep on with my eyes cast down, my gaze averted from everything that might deter me from my fevered course. Consumed by this narrowed obsessive part of myself, I won't listen to what the whole person in me knows to be true. I stubbornly persevere.

Pride engenders all the poisoned fruits of sin that ripen in the disintegrating personality: lies, false accusations, self-pity, angry attacks on the innocent, icy sarcasm, mean cruelties. A person may indulge in "silent tantrums," cutting off and rejecting others through obdurate silence. As sin produces more inner chaos and the person seeks to confuse others, he or she will totally disregard truth and reality, and say anything or do anything to protect the self and its sin. Self-disgusted, but still self-indulgent, one begins to see others as false and weak; cynicism about oneself produces distrust and arrogance toward others. If everyone is corrupt, who could ask anything more of me? To ensure my moral security system, I gradually begin to avoid my more virtuous friends and find myself gravitating toward those I can look down upon, if not despise.

The clinical psychological literature on the way a person defends the self from painful reality is heartily confirmed by our common human experience of sin. The worse the moral state, the more fragile, defensive, and stubborn we become. How often we catch ourselves in the self-protective process of self-deception, yet go on to harden our heart and blind our eyes to the truth. The operation of personal conscience may be mostly a matter of decisions made in fleeting moments. Are we going to recognize reality and focus on our failure, or are we going to choose denial and self-deception by rushing to sweep away what troubles us. The scriptural description of how sinners hate the light and cling to the darkness is an apt depiction of the psychological strategies we use to avoid the light of self-awareness.

RECOGNIZING SIN

After we have had experiences of sin, recognized our self-ensnarement, and repented, we can note the same insidious processes of sin in others. Since we judge ourselves, we cannot help evaluating the failures of others. Knowledge of good and evil and personal experience inevitably propels us into critical moral evaluations. A capacity to evaluate self and others by standards of goodness or excellence emerges in every child during the second or third year—along with the universal emotions of guilt, contempt, and shame. The human animal is innately equipped with something no other species possesses, the ability to acquire and apply standards of morality or achievement in judgments of self and others. Self-evaluation emerges in all children.

This programmed appearance of guilt, shame, and contempt, combined with a loving attachment to caretakers, makes the moral socialization of human beings possible. The child's emerging evaluative abilities make possible instruction in the particular norms, ideals, and taboos of family and community. When a beloved mother is upset and censures a child's attack on a baby sister, the child is inwardly ready to agree, to feel fear of abandonment and guilt over the wrongdoing. After years of being properly brought up, we know moral failure when we see it in ourselves and others.

We become particularly adept at judging the inner motivation of those whom we know well. Unfortunately, this means that we can be most aware of the sins of those we are closest to—the very sins that will pain us most deeply. Persons whom we consistently observe at close range, with whom we have established empathetic connections, are the very ones we can most clearly see sinning. Knowing what their own standards are and what they hold to be wrong, we can see them turn away from the demands of conscience; we watch them give in to pride, selfish desire, or lying defenses, although we know they know better. Our very closeness to them gives us a penetrating view of the way they are morally failing. In the case of more distant acquaintances the evaluation might be more tentative, since their inner life may be more obscure.

When we love a person, the sorrow of seeing them sin, even if it is not wronging us, can be most upsetting. Sometimes, we can't face the fact, and we end up colluding with them in order to deny what is really happening. Here the psychological observation that in many cases there exists an "enabler" who continually contributes to another's weakness, is an accurate one. Good nurturing persons do enable others to continue to drink, or lie, or abuse the innocent, or shirk responsibilities and the painful consequences of their actions. By acquiescing and covering up, by smoothing over and perpetually picking up the pieces, good people can enable their loved ones to continue sinning in ways they would not tolerate in others. With those we dislike, our eyes are unforgivingly clear and our anger easily aroused.

Our innate predisposition to be moral comes with an equally natural bent for moral indignation. A child's first protest comes early; "But it isn't fair!" (often our last deathbed cry as well). And a child's protests are never limited simply to selfish concerns. A human being possesses innately programmed empathy from the beginning; small children are unhappy when others are hurt or sad. Natural empathy, developing into sympathy, urges us to try to right wrongs and help our fellow creatures. Altruism—the tendency to act unselfishly for the good of another—is as much an inherited predisposition from the selective evolution of the species, as our less attractive human tendencies to selfishness, aggression and self-deceit. People seem programmed to leap into altruistic acts without a moment's thought. This altruistic bent to relieve and rescue our fellows develops into a powerful natural wish that righteousness prevail. The need to see the good victorious and wrongdoers vanquished has from time immemorial fueled folktales, myths, epics, and ritual dramas. From childhood on, we are ready (all too ready) to demolish the sinner. Admonishing the sinner may take a great deal more restraint.

ADMONISHING: DISTINCTIONS AND CONSIDERATIONS

Distinctions have to be made when considering what admonishing the sinner involves. What are the limits and boundaries of admonishing? What should the motivation be and what emotional costs are involved? Only after these questions are addressed can the complexities of practical ways and means of admonishment be considered. Of course no blueprints can be drawn for what must be a unique personal encounter, but some rough guidelines may be formulated.

If we begin with our tendency toward moral indignation and the temptation to destroy the wicked, we have to ask how admonishing the sinner differs from an attack or from judgmental condemnation? And at the opposite end of the spectrum of human feeling, the question arises as to how admonishing differs from parental nagging? To admonish, according to the dictionary, means "to remind, to warn of a fault, to reprove gently or kindly, but seriously; to exhort, also to put one in mind of something forgotten by way of warning or exhortation." So defined, admonishing another, cannot be the same as attacking, condemning, or harshly judging. Such hostile acts are not gentle or kind reminders.

Condemnations and judgments decisively end an interpersonal transaction; there is nothing more to be done or said after a denunciation of past misbehavior. Hostile reactions directed to what has been done already, are neither future-oriented nor hopeful. A warning or exhortation should involve an evaluation of present behavior; it should be directed to the future and positive change. And the future envisioned is a shared one, otherwise we would not take the trouble to warn; we would just condemn, shake the dust from our feet, and move on. When we exhort or remind we are not making final judgments, separating ourselves from the sinner as the sheep are separated from the goats or as Lazarus in Abraham's bosom is separated from the rich man in hell.

Admonishing resembles nagging, but there is a difference. Admonishments of sin are more serious, therefore less frequently given. They aim at reminding someone of what he or she prefers to forget and are not specifically aimed at controlling another's behavior. By contrast, in nagging a specific behavior is spelled out and reiterated—again and again and again. Of course I am nagging you for your own good, but my need to have you conform to my will for your own good can gradually become stronger than my desire for your well-being. In contrast, when I admonish you I bring a serious matter involving your conscience to your attention. As I confront, remind, exhort, and warn you, I can only appeal to your inner heart and mind to freely choose another course. Since a sin is, by definition, a matter of your free personal will and exercise of conscience, I have to leave you with your own moral responsibility for your future action. Merely submitting to my control or conforming to my blueprint for your behavior won't work.

Reflecting upon the complexity of this, it seems clear that I should not admonish another until I have searched my own heart. Admonishing should not be a way of manipulating another and exerting external controls. I also have to be sure that I am not up to the old trick of projecting my flaws on you, of seeing the mote in your eye while ignoring the beam in my own. We all have a tendency to notice in others those flaws that we are either tempted toward or are already indulging ourselves. If our vigilant conscience is bent on self-correction, it is also sensitized to those personal weaknesses we have *not* eradicated, and thus our attention is drawn like a magnet to those same failings in others. If I relish the thought of admonishing you, finally controlling you, something may be amiss. I need to stop and examine my motives and goals.

LOVE IS THE MOTIVE FOR ADMONISHING

Ultimately love is the only acceptable motive and goal for acts of admonishment. Love not only comforts, but also discomfits in its commitment to truth and reality. In the end we admonish one another in love because God, Jesus, and the saints and prophets have given us their example of admonishing love. If I care about you and your ultimate good, I will tell you what you would rather not hear, even at the risk of pain, trouble, and your rejection of me. I warn you, remind you, and exhort you for your own sake and for the common good of the community we share.

If I believe that sin leads us away from the love of God and neighbor, I can only be saddened to see you moving away from love and truth—and happiness as well. Sin not only does grievous harm to others; it also makes the sinner miserable. Contrary to popular misconception, and with only rare exceptions, there are few serene and joyful sinners. Sin withers and stunts the spirit. Thrashing about in its snare, lying and blaming to defend and protect one's sin, a person not mentally ill enters upon a preview of purgatory and hell. Hell can begin here and now, as one rejects truth and love and separates one's self from God. The great Teresa of Avila correctly said that all the way to heaven is heaven; and the obverse is also true: all the way to hell is hell. We are daily constructing our future: either we choose life or we choose death and gloom.

ATTACHMENT AND SUFFERING

If I love you I want you to be happy, to flourish, to be moving and enspirited. I can't stand to see you falling apart and spiraling downward to spiritual destruction and death-in-life. Thus I admonish you, urging you to turn again and live. When I care about you, I am emotionally involved in our common future. Here Christianity parts company with other more stoic forms of spirituality that emphasize psychological detachment. Yes, one can control one's personal suffering by resolutely pursuing detachment from desire and human bonds, as the ancient wisdom asserts. Some modern self-help strategies are modeled on ancient blueprints for gaining psychological peace through detachment and a rational mastery of the self.

True, you can change no one's life but your own, and, yes, we ultimately die alone. Assuredly, no person can make another person happy. Marcus Aurelius was correct when he said, "to live happily is an inward power of the soul." The person or soul who turns inward through stoic discipline and self-mastery can become invulnerable to reversals of fortune, disease, death, losses, or human betrayal. But this does not seem the Christian way, which insists that love and desires for mutual happiness with others must be fulfilled in communal bonds. The Kingdom of God must come for us all. Christians can never give each other up. If being involved in others' failures through love and caring brings us personal suffering, so be it. We follow a crucified God, who truly suffered for love rather than retreat to the power of unmoved self-sufficiency and detachment.

For Christians, suffering in this world is not illusory because the individual selves that suffer are not illusory. Our human emotions of love, desire, and sorrow are reflections of the divine persons of the Trinity, not traps to be overcome on the way to Nirvana or to the ultimate unity of all with all. Concern and sorrow over the sins and failings of those we love arise from our deep emotional involvement with them. Efforts must be made to bring them to the communal feast; we must admonish sinners if we love them.

MODES OF ADMONISHMENT

To admonish sinners we have to be as wise as a serpent and as innocent as a dove. It is important to discriminate among the different relationships we have with others. Public persons and those in institutional roles may need to be admonished in special ways. From ancient times there has been a tradition of prophets who admonish leaders and their people. What is different today is the conscious development of effective strategies to be used in collective nonviolent resistance movements. Gandhi and Martin Luther King, Jr., were masters of seizing the right moment and devising appropriate actions. What is effective at one historical moment for Solidarity members in Poland, may or may not be appropriate in the Philippine struggle against oppressive authorities. Our American efforts to exhort and admonish sinners will be shaped by our traditions of freedom and civil liberties—whether within or outside of the Church. Unfortunately, a closer look at such political movements is beyond the scope of our present discussion of individual behavior.

Complex discriminations are called for in our immediate circles. Employers, professional colleagues, pastors, fellow parishioners, community leaders, and local acquaintances present challenges different from those of our family, close colleagues, and friends. Relevant variables seem to be the intimacy, commitment, and power involved in a relationship. Power comes into the picture in two ways. The more power a person has over me, the more difficult, but therefore the more necessary, it is for me to have the courage to admonish them. Those above me in any particular power structure will need me to warn them, for others may cravenly acquiesce or accommodate the boss, the chairman, the rich donor, the pastor, the bishop, or whatever. When private, tactful wise-as-serpents strategies don't get through, one has to meditate on John the Baptist and courageously wade into deeper, riskier waters.

When power runs the other way and I must admonish those with less power than myself, other standards should be applied. Even if my role involves admonishing, I should be slow to do so to those under my authority. God is slow to anger and full of heartfelt mercy and gracious kindness, and so should we be. One swallow does not make a summer, and one lapse would not need admonishment; warnings are only appropriate for repeated, ongoing sins. If a person has repented, he or she by definition no longer needs admonitions or exhortations to remind them of the sin. Did the prodigal son's father deliver dire warnings about future dangers to be avoided, or does the shepherd beat the lost sheep after finding it? Persons who repent need joyful acceptance that conveys the sense of trust that the future will be different. Anxious advice about avoiding sin is a form of debilitating nagging and implies that a person can't cope or change.

Another important discrimination to be made in admonishments is how intimate I am, and how fully I share commitments, with the erring person. Christ admonished his own more freely, as did Paul and other Christians throughout history. If we are all climbing the same mountain, roped together for support, I am much more concerned and obliged to point out your false footing or your dangerous move toward the edge of the ravine. I need your strength more and I care more intensely because if you fall we all go down. Since so much is at stake in our common journey, it is even harder for me to avoid anger when I must admonish you. As family life, civil wars, and all close communities demonstrate, love and hate are more closely related than love and indifference. Caring so much and on so many different levels, I have to be more reflective and self-testing before I speak.

MEANS OF ADMONISHING

Sometimes, of course, we can admonish without speaking. We are able to communicate through deeds and nonverbal channels—in a glance, touch, gesture, pose, or facial expression. Christ's gaze at Peter after his betrayal was a powerful admonishment. So, too, in another way was Christ's washing of his disciples' feet. Gestures along with silence can also speak, as when Christ silently bent down to write in the dirt while a mob raged to stone the woman taken in adultery. In a sense, one's whole life with all its deeds gives more of a message than any word of direct exhortation. This is why the innocent and good are routinely hated by the evil. They are perceived as admonishing others by their example, even when they do not intend to. On the other hand, if one's own deeds contradict an admonishment given others, the hypocrisy cancels the effect of speaking. Again, before acting one must look to one's self.

Once one decides to speak in admonishment, all the workshops or self-help books on communication can be put to good use. These "human relations skills" are justly judged to be superficial, in that they cannot tell you what to say, but they can help in effectively getting a message across. They rightly emphasize choosing a favorable time and place, being aware of one's tone of voice, eye contact, posture, as well as clear wording. Obviously, you can never communicate with others unless you first have their attention. Then, of course, you have to put your message in comprehensible language that will not immediately alienate your listeners. As Paul attests, to the Greeks you must be as a Greek, fitting your words "to the needs of each one." After all, in the Incarnation God reaches out to us humans in a way that we can grasp, so an emphasis upon the medium as the message cannot be all wrong. How we say something, whether gently, kindly, or considerately, delivers a large part of the message. Human beings operate and communicate on many levels, and the emotional exchange in any encounter is as important as the linguistic meanings.

An indirect approach through a teaching story is also a powerful means of communication. Stories are effective because they combine emotionally engrossing narratives with meanings given on different levels at once. The hearer must discover the message through personal emotional response. The prophet Nathan tells King David a story and gets his admonishment across. David responds to the injustice detailed and recognizes his own sinful behavior in a sudden insight. Christ constantly uses parables to warn and admonish—the man building his house upon the sand, the burying of talents, the foolish virgins, and so on. In imaginative sensitive listeners, the use of imagery in a story awakens heart and mind. Defensive obduracy is outwitted: I become engaged in the story and before I can harden my mind and heart to the message that is coming, the moral challenge hooks me. Such great teaching stories exist in many different religious traditions and their powerful images refuse to fade away. Similarly, a story told by a reformed sinner is a powerful method of admonishment. It works wonders in Alcoholics Anonymous and other self-help groups because it gives hope for future happiness through the amendment of one's life.

When, however, admonishment invokes anxiety and fear, the results are likely to be negative. Crime-prevention programs that take juvenile delinquents on tours of prisons have been found to be counterproductive. Fear and anxiety can lead to despair that makes one give up in powerless hope-lessness. Lurid sermons on hell and the damnation of sinners were surely equally wrongheaded, wronghearted, and may have led to many sins. Anxiety brings about the feared thing, but love casts out fear and encourages hope. Admonishments will be most effective when love and imagination are used to enlarge the heart and hold up the hope for a more abundant life. Getting to a better and more joyful future with God is what admonishment is all about. Admonishing the sinner is an effort to liberate another through Christ's saving power of love.

AFTERMATHS

If an admonishment has been done in love and done wisely, it will have intrinsic value whether or not it has practical effects for the sinner's behavior. One who admonishes bears witness to community and caring for a unique person, as well as to the importance of religious and moral values. To admonish you I must observe you and take your conscience seriously. Even if I must suffer for what I see as a spiritual response to a need, I have not wasted my pain in a trivial cause. Besides, a momentary or temporary rejection may not be the end of the story. Sometimes a saddening break leads to much more solid relations in the future.

It really does happen sometimes, that a worried-over admonition has an almost miraculous effect. I know a man, a faithful member of Alcoholics Anonymous, who feared he would lose his job by confronting and admonishing his employer with the diagnosis of early-stage alcoholism that was bringing harm to himself, his family, and his business. The employer responded with instant assent and that day stopped drinking. His inner struggles and troubled conscience were triggered into repentance and reform by the tactful, loving admonition of his friend and employee. The extra pressure of an outsider can sometimes be the deciding factor in an inner battle. Such instant feedback for one's effort to reach out to another is rare.

In any event, our charge is to love and respond to a need, even if we cannot guarantee the success of our actions. I must do my part as wisely and as well as I can, and leave the outcome to God.

CONCLUSION

To admonish the sinner is to remind a person, who needs to be reminded, of what he or she already knows in conscience. One calls a person back to a better self, to a whole self with its need for integrity and honor, its need to be true to past aspirations and present standards of conscience. To admonish is to call a person to attention, to serve as a loving witness for the better future with Christ that is presently being negated. One is not really intruding, condescending, or condemning but rather helping another, as one in turn needs to be helped.

When I become mired in self-imposed blindness and inertia I can all too easily avoid recognizing that I am clinging to my sins, despite the harm they bring to me and those around me. When you graciously confront me face to face, I must face the reality of my failure. I need your witness and support. Only through the truth can I become truly free. If we don't care enough, or have courage enough, to admonish one another's sins, we fail in love.

2

TO INSTRUCT THE IGNORANT

Fill your minds with everything that is true, everything that is noble, everything that is good and pure, everything that we love and honor, and everything that can be thought virtuous or worthy of praise. Keep doing all the things that you learned from me and have been taught by me and have heard or seen that I do. (Philippians 4:8)

The life and death of each of us has its influence on others. (Romans 14:7)

What is ignorance? And what does it have to do with us? Why should we go about correcting it? The essence of ignorance seems to be a failing to notice, and then failing to notice that we fail to notice. The worst thing about ignorance is that one can remain smugly, blissfully unaware of it. If you already know that you don't know, if you are aware of your own ignorance, you have made the first great leap toward knowledge. Unfortunately, unless another person cares enough to instruct you, you can remain blind, dumb, and ignorant until you die.

Persons instruct those who are ignorant for all sorts of reasons. Secular self-interest is one great motivator. Who wants to live and work with those who know nothing? Every functioning society needs to educate its new members in order to survive. If our tribe lives by hunting and we fail to teach the young to hunt, then we will all die of hunger when the present generation of hunters grows old. And if a civilized community is wanted, then the general populace must be educated and instructed to a civilized standard. Gone are the days when powerful elites could withdraw to their protected preserves and count on safety for themselves and their children. Today, in our increasingly complex and technological world, we have to recognize our interdependence and mutual vulnerability. The ignorance of some can threaten the welfare of all. Nowadays, at the very least, someone has to be paid to educate and civilize the plebeian mobs. Barbarians within the gates can create too much havoc and destruction.

But the act of instructing the ignorant can be motivated by active love as a spiritual or personal work of mercy. The desire to instruct and relieve ignorance can spring from far more than self-interest. Even if I am not threatened by another person's limited development, when I love a human person I naturally want them to be all that they can be. I want it for their own sake, and I want it because I can't stand the waste of godgiven human potential. If we love the world and the people in it, we want to see the full flowering of all human talents. Most of all I want those ignorant of the good news of the Gospel to be liberated from the land of gloom. After all, God has created us and instructed us out of love. Jesus spent his ministry instructing his followers and inspiring them to learn from him. Should we not in our gratitude do the same for others?

When we feel grateful to those who have instructed us, we long to go and instruct others in the same way. We seem naturally impelled to give what we have received, to imitate the models we admire. Look at the child carefully giving her doll tender maternal care and lessons in good behavior. Filial piety has been considered a basic virtue and foundation of civilization because it encourages the gratitude to one's progenitors that motivates similar caregiving and instruction for the next generation. And fortunately, instruction is never just a one-way process, since when we teach we also learn. Gratitude initiates ongoing links of mutual instruction that go on forever. Life is a great school, in which we alternate the roles of student and instructor.

We can hardly avoid constant teaching and learning in all the domains of life. Human beings are organisms programmed to learn and communicate. It is the innate nature of *Homo sapiens* to want to seek truth, solve problems, and pass on the knowledge. As the rational animal, we are made in the image of a God who is infinite truth, the inexhaustible creative source of reality. Persons seek truth to fulfill their deep innate hunger to know. We want to know more and more, because there is always more to know. But the search for knowledge begins with an acceptance of our present ignorance. The more there is yet to be known, the more ignorance there must exist here and now.

One can be ignorant of culture, art, literature, logic, mathematics, and the world of science. One can lack social and political understanding of the way one's world functions. One can be ignorant of psychology and of one's self, and one can be ignorant of religion, God, and God's dealings with human beings. All of these forms of ignorance have much in common. And all processes of instruction—education, therapy, and religious instruction—are also similar. Teachers, missionaries, therapists, and parents find that they all do much the same thing in similar ways. Certain truths about teaching and instructing apply generally. But here I shall emphasize religious, psychological, and social instruction as being more personal, more motivated by active love, and, so, more prototypically spiritual.

True ignorance does not really signify a simple lack of information or facts. To repeat what was said above, ignorance is always much more serious than not having a set of facts on hand. If one knows what information one does not have, then one will have some idea of how to get it, and the battle is almost won. Real ignorance consists of not knowing that we don't know and, therefore, having no idea of how to go about finding out something that we do not even know exists to be found. The young Helen Keller was blind, deaf, and dumb and could not at first imagine that there was such a thing as language to be learned and used for personal communication. Once she grasped the miraculous concept that words could signify things, that her own primary experience of "water" could be named and communicated, her life was changed forever. Learning an innumerable number of specific new words was easy compared to her first great abstract discovery of the general principle of naming things. The gratitude Helen felt to her teacher who liberated her from dumb ignorance, lasted for the rest of her life.

But Helen's teacher did not penetrate Helen's ignorance easily. This long-ago struggle of a teacher to instruct a small handicapped child in rural Alabama has been dramatized often on stage and screen over the years and has moved millions of people. This conflict between a child's self-willed ignorance and her teacher's determination to teach, has the power of an epic, because it embodies the paradoxical challenge of instructing the ignorant. In human beings an innate thirst to learn coexists with a deep resistance to submitting one's self to the new and alien perspective of teachers who make new demands. While all children possess a natural curiosity, they also possess a bull-headed determination to do things their own way. Like many grown-ups, children can feel deep shame and humiliation when they must admit and confront their own ignorance. Self-protective strategies to avoid pain can stubbornly resist all enlightenment. Apathy and the cooling of the desire to know is one defense that can begin fairly early.

More pain can arise from the discipline and hard work it takes to learn to master something. Just as it takes patience and effort to teach, so it takes effort and patience to learn. If shame and impatience and the need to avoid pain and failure dominate, the will to learn may be dulled (if never totally extinguished). The art of teaching begins with the ability to outwit and minimize the pain and shame that can emerge in the student's confrontation with ignorance and failed attempts at mastery. Logically, it should be no shame to be ignorant. How could a person possibly know something without prior instruction or experience? But with proud sensitive human beings, shame at nonculpable, unavoidable ignorance seems inevitable. Adam and Eve became newly ashamed of their nakedness after they tasted evil in the garden. God grieved over the shame and fear that accompanied the Fall: "Who told you, you were naked?" Alas, human pride produces shame, shame produces fear, and fear casts out love and brings more shame—the enemies of truth flourish. To be able to learn about reality, one has to cease being afraid of confronting what one doesn't know.

INSTRUCTING AND INSTRUCTORS

All who wish to instruct the ignorant must overcome the paradox. A teacher, therapist, parent, or missionary knows something, and knows, too, that the other person does not know; while the other may be shamed to feel ignorant, he or she is also motivated by the innate human thirst for truth and reality. Neither the knowledge of another's relative ignorance, nor the student's innate desire and ability to learn can be ignored. A teacher must keep both of these things in mind. In our democratic times some persons overzealous for equality have resisted any recognition of ignorance and incompetence; they refuse to accept as a reality that the teacher, parent, or therapist must in some sense know more than the one who needs to be instructed. They confound our godgiven intrinsic equality as human beings with our inevitably unequal status as beginning, intermediate, or advanced students in some field. Yes, we are all learning together and we always learn from each other, but those who instruct should have advanced farther than those instructed.

At the other extreme are those instructors who refuse to believe in the inner ally and the intrinsic universal desire of human beings to learn and to grow. They refuse to build on the positive with praise and gentle encouragement. Some instructors will even champion the fear of punishment and anxiety as the only reliable human motivators. Others will defend an elite view of instruction, and regard only a few talented persons as teachable. Elitists would do well to study infants and observe the intense interest and desire of infants to learn about the world. Piaget described the infant as behaving like a small scientist in the crib, seeking, exploring, and trying to understand. More recent investigators of infancy have been even more astounded at the infant's abilities and desires from birth to encounter and understand reality. Infants do not start out in a hazy world of wish fulfillment, but with an orientation to seek and master the truth of things. When we instruct the ignorant, we should never collude with their ignorance, nor should we ever underestimate innate human abilities to learn and to grow. Our hopes for successful instructing are well-grounded in human nature.

Perhaps we teach best by keeping in touch with our own past experiences of moving from ignorance to knowledge. We can remember the joy of learning something, the intrinsic delight of mastery and new recognition of our own developing understanding and competence. Often—as, say, in learning to ride a bike—there is a long frustrating struggle, followed by a moment when we finally get it. This sudden grasp of the integrated process as a whole—of the big picture or the necessary solution—has been called the "aha" or "eureka" experience. This epiphany, or sudden rush of enlightenment or mastery, is so delightful that we forever seek its repetition through different activities. Sports, games, puzzles, riddles, jokes, crossword puzzles, and the life of the mind and science attract us because we love and adore the high of finally seeing some solution or discovering a relationship, of suddenly being able to "get it."

When we can enable another to feel this mastery, we experience their glow of success vicariously. When we help another "get it," whatever "it" happens to be, we are doubly delighted. We are catapulted back to our original good feeling when we first learned it, and we have the second experience of competence in now having successfully passed it on. A parent runs along behind the bike and finally sees the child ride away unassisted by the helping hand, no longer needing the lessons on how to balance, "that's right, go a little faster, turn into the fall." This moment of mutual triumph is a simple demonstration of what a privilege it is to teach anyone anything. The patient effort involved in instruction is rewarded a thousand times over.

Each of us can remember many such breakthroughs into mastery or insight, compounded by the later joy of passing them on to others. To this day I remember learning to tie my shoes at age four. What a triumph it was to finally succeed after the repeated frustrations of this seemingly impossible task. When the time came to teach my own children to tie their shoes I remembered my own pain—and eventual victory. To teach a child to master a complex task of daily life is indeed an achievement. The great genius Maria Montessori understood both how to teach and the joy of teaching. She was the first to systematically provide materials and a structured environment in which children could more easily master reality—child-sized furniture, rods that demonstrate fractions, large sandpaper letters. To teach another person to cook, to wash dishes, to sew, to read—any of the skills and competencies that our complicated world demands—gives riches to another. And how satisfying it is also to teach of intellectual, psychological, and spiritual matters, which are even more complex, subtle and uniquely personal.

The art of instruction is based upon the teacher's ability to put the self in the other's place and see the situation as they see it. I can only lead another to a new place if I can enter the place where he or she now is and get them to accompany me on the journey. I must cultivate the ability to jump back and forth from my perspective and goals, to the student's point of view. These mediating perspectives will have to shift constantly in the course of progress. Instructing in all its forms necessitates the double vision, how to be teacher and one's student at the same time. Empathy and the ability to take the role of the other while maintaining one's own perspective produce an effective teacher, parent, therapist, missionary—or savior. The Incarnation is the supreme model of effective mediation and instruction.

Teaching is best done by those who love their students for love induces the attention, empathy, encouraging praise, and perseverance necessary to penetrate the other person's perspective and move the other toward the common goal. Hate, vengeance, and the desire to control or break a person may inspire equally keen attentiveness, but since the goal of hate can never be a mutual good, the victim's resistance may eventually sabotage the enterprise. A successful teacher perseveres out of goodwill toward the student; the teacher's respect for the student and their mutual goal help overcome shame, fear of failure, distrust, and apathetic indifference. A teacher who loves and cares enough to pay a student sustained attention can be inspired to hit upon what will work to instruct this learner in this situation at this moment. One may always look for a "teaching moment," but the good teacher specializes in making such moments happen. What will work here and now?

Love and goodwill sustain hope for future success. If a teacher gives up in despair before starting, progress is impossible. We know now from a great deal of psychological research the enormous influence of expectancy. Those students who are expected to learn, will learn. What a teacher expects to happen shapes the outcome. If a teacher is impatient and quick to disparage, only the very quickest students will learn—and they will learn arrogant impatience along with the lesson. A discouraging impression will be made, namely, that only the most able are worth expenditures of time and effort. How different from that most loving teacher who proclaims, "a bruised reed I will not break nor a flickering wick extinguish." Since God is love, and pays constant attention, the Holy One is the supremely patient teacher. Loving patience and hope are all-important in teaching, therapy, and parenthood. Knowledge is a necessary but not sufficient condition. A good teacher or therapist or parent must be able to imagine change, inspire change, and shrewdly gauge what will make it happen.

All change has been described as a process of unfreezing, reforming and refreezing. The first stage of unfreezing, or stirring up the status quo, must take place before any new learning begins. Something must happen to stimulate a learner to focus attention, and see the inadequacy or insufficiency of the existing state of affairs. Some awareness of need, ignorance, or incompleteness has to emerge before movement is motivated. The tendency toward inertia and stasis can be disturbed by some crisis or, at the other extreme, some positive force may enter the field and induce a desire or readiness for something new and better, some awakening of the innate desire to learn more.

After instruction and learning takes place, the new patterns will soon have to withstand the counterpressure for a regression to the old status quo. In the terms of the Gospel we would say that all newly sown seed will be in danger of being choked by the return of perennial weeds. Old habits and old ways will reassert themselves. Whenever a functioning system is disturbed it tries to reestablish equilibrium. No person can have freedom diminished without some reaction aimed at reasserting the old liberty. Thus, for successful change or learning, a refreezing stage is necessary so that what one has learned is assimilated and becomes more than a temporary exercise or enthusiasm. A good instructor will try to prepare a learner for the prolonged practice necessary for new learning to really take hold. One must prepare learners for obstacles and lengthy efforts. Good teachers who love their students are interested in the long run and long-term results.

The best teachers aim to give their students ways to learn for themselves. Never give a hungry man a fish when you can teach him how to fish. The golden rule of all instruction is to become biodegradable, to pass on a self-generating process so that one's teaching is no longer needed. Every good teacher, therapist, or parent wants to induce self-guidance. Now that I've shown you why and how, go and do what you have seen me do. In Christianity we have the model of Jesus, who promised his disciples that they would do even greater works than he, after he departed. He told his followers to learn from him and sent them out to the harvest. Christians are charged to grow up into the fullness of Jesus, to be adult friends, not perpetual children. A loving teacher, therapist, or missionary wants to lead those they instruct into full equality. One starts out with inequality and ignorance and moves the learner into equality and, if possible, toward greater achievements than one's own.

In the course of becoming unnecessary instructors must prepare their students to always look for what is not obvious. One of the most important things that one can teach another is to pursue an awareness of the hidden frameworks and prior assumptions which may be constricting one's vision or confining one's range of solutions. Again this means that in overcoming ignorance we don't solely work on learning bit by bit, but focus attention instead on the process: What are the guiding principles, presumptions, and goals which will shape the larger picture? In other words, one of the most important things to inspire is the student's future search for what I don't yet know that I don't know. Humility and openness to new and different ways of seeing become the best educational policy. Socrates always spoke of his lack of knowledge and proceeded to become one of the greatest teachers of all time— without publishing a word.

While all successful teachers have much in common as they pursue the essentials, it is also the case that a variety of individual styles will flourish. Consider the great teachers, therapists, or parents that one has known, they are alike in some essentials and yet also had different talents. A variety of teaching styles can work together, much as different instruments in the orchestra can carry the same musical theme; indeed, different individuals at different times in their lives may respond best to many different approaches. Let a thousand flowers bloom seems the general rule of good instruction. All flowering species share the common processes of photosynthesis and reproduction, but there can be riotous differences in color, shape, and scent. Getting the most productive match between individual learner and individual teacher is sometimes a challenge, whether in school, therapy or religious direction.

One interesting typology of instructors can be constructed from an analogy with tribal healers in different cultures. Among many tribes in different lands one finds the recurring figures of the shaman, magician, naturalist, priest, or mystic healer. With their different methods, they can all produce change in an individual. Shamans operate with a sense of personal power, conviction, autonomy, and faith in themselves, along with a certain potential for narcissism and megalomania. Shamans bring about change on the basis of their personal influence and power, their ability to induce trust in their power. Magicians, naturalists, and priests do not rely on personal influence but on their accrued knowledge, or positions as gatekeepers.

None of the changes that shaman, magician, naturalist, or priest can bring about can match the effects wrought by the mystic healers. The mystic healer, like a good teacher, is a catalyst for change and instructs as a form of love and personal investment in the other's well-being. In contrast to the more superficial self-centered endeavors of the other types of wonder-workers, mystic healers inspire learning as a means for the other person's unique integration and fulfillment. Unlike shamans or magicians, mystic healers are those teachers who, while they may be dramatic and colorful, still do not rely upon quick tricks or props, and they seek no permanent dependents. The lessons learned from these good teachers are both simple and profound, and last for a lifetime. Mystic healers also appear in an amazing diversity, from Zen Buddhist monks to the devoted schoolmarms who populate American autobiographies. They, along with great therapists and great parents, have the power to inspire growth and integration, invoking feelings of gratitude. Like Socrates, effective instructors are unafraid of their own ignorance, and insist that their students seek to know themselves.

PSYCHOLOGICAL AND SPIRITUAL INSTRUCTION OF THE IGNORANT

But what of these even more subtle realms of psychological and spiritual instruction? How do we teach others to know themselves, or begin religious instruction about God's ways with human beings? Heretofore, the family has always been the first and most primary school for the development of character and religious understanding. But instruction continues in many different kinds of situations encountered throughout a lifetime. Parents teach their children about God and the self, but so do siblings, peers, teachers, therapists, clergy, employers, fellow workers, lovers, mates, and the family one creates as an adult. The development of the self is lifelong and emerges as the one necessary, unavoidable curriculum. Even those who have avoided or been denied all formal religious or psychological instruction will have to enter this school. When people talk about the school of hard knocks, they are referring to the fact that life is a long process of overcoming, or failing to overcome, self-ignorance and self-delusion. Today in secular circles the task which religions and spiritual counselors were traditionally assigned is often given to psychology and therapy. But the perennial questions and dilemmas remain and reappear to give trouble.

Why are we so ignorant and easily deceived about ourselves? Why don't we achieve self-knowledge more promptly? Although philosophers and mystics have always said that spiritual progress requires self-knowledge, the task remains incredibly difficult. We look around us and see such widespread blindness to self—and, of course, we have had enough painful personal experiences of entrapment in illusion and ignorance of self to recognize the condition. Intense new interest in this ancient human problem has produced a provocative new psychology of self-deception.

According to some new theories self-deception is genetically programmed into the human species. Some measure of self-deception has adaptive uses that favor its continued use in the struggle for human survival. Persons who can successfully fool themselves, may look more sincere to others, seem more sincere to themselves, and so be able to garner more of the environment's resources; they can rationalize their selfish strategies and provide advantages to their own offspring, who perpetuate the genes. Evolutionary theorists are just as sure that altruism, cooperation, and learning are also innate, so one finds a curious secular replay of original-sin theories in which human nature is mostly good, but also wounded in its propensity for self-enhancing illusions.

Other investigations of self-deception do not focus on evolutionary strategies but upon the way human consciousness functions day to day. A built-in need for self-deception is posited as emerging from the strong human drive to avoid pain and seek pleasure. Avoiding pain by not attending to it may be both an innate and learned defensive strategy. There may be physical and psychological trade-offs and adjustments between pain and attention. If I don't notice something, it hurts less; it is easier to avoid a painful reality than try to change it. The self's negative experiences of weakness, failure, and wrongdoing may be particularly painful to confront with full awareness, ergo a defensive dimming of attention or out-right avoidance becomes the best defense.

Self-scrutiny and introspection have traditionally been known as painful and difficult enterprises. Research studies of attention and self-consciousness have confirmed the fact that when we become self-conscious we usually become self-crit-ical. Our attention is turned inward upon our weaknesses and inadequacies, we notice our failures to meet our own stan-dards. Pain and the threat to our self-esteem tempt us defen-sively to change or distort reality in order to be able to protect ourselves from the truth. We can learn to keep our attention dimmed or turned outward in habitual defensive strategies that prevent self-knowledge.

Habitual self-deception is possible because humans have multiple, complex, different levels of functioning and con-sciousness. Highly differentiated semi-independent systems are an advantage when it comes to self-correction; one system can check, substitute for, or correct the input of another. But it is also possible for systems to become isolated or fail to be integrated properly. We usually function with several simul-taneously interacting systems—with a physiological system, an emotional-affective interpersonal system, and a conscious-rational symbolic system. Each system contributes to a sense of self or identity. The most familiar self that we recognize is the alert awake consciousness or "I" that seems to scan the world without and within like a narrow beam of light. When we daydream or go to sleep we can feel this beam fading and other levels of functioning taking over. When awake we direct our beam of attentive consciousness toward reality, ready to cope with daily life.

But when our coping is not successful or when we are frustrated, we can see defensive maneuvers taking place in consciousness and attention. Our dedication to reality wavers, particularly if self-scrutiny is in order. We resist turning the light inward upon ourselves because of the discomfort and critical function of self-consciousness. The habitual defensive strategies can begin. Because we are so complicated it seems possible that information can be processed but remain isolated from full conscious awareness. We become adept at hiding from full self-confrontation, in order to avoid pain, procure pleasure or block the moral self-censure of guilt or shame. The more maladaptive the process becomes and the more we hide from self-knowledge, the more threatened and defensive we become.

All psychological therapies or programs for self-knowledge or spiritual disciplines insist upon directing consciousness inward in searching self-observation. This mindfulness or sustained attention to inner reality is a painful but necessary discipline for personal change and progress. The natural tendency toward self-deception and defense has to be struggled against by equally strong efforts toward reality and truthful self-confrontation. When a person's automatic, heretofore avoided or isolated defensive processes are attended to and brought to full consciousness, a person can be free to choose in new ways what will determine his or her future life. We are told to know ourselves so that we can be freed from being driven by hidden forces with which we have colluded in self-protective strategies of self-deception. Naturally we resist the pain and the effort to overcome ignorance of the self, even while desiring to be free.

We both seek and resist enlightenment, but without the help of other persons we can never overcome self-deception. No one can experience themselves or see themselves as others do. We cannot see how we look from the back, or be fully conscious of all our unconscious habits and mannerisms, nor can we penetrate our personality all by ourselves. Others must disclose us to ourselves by their response to us. One can overcome ignorance of the self by the ongoing dialogue with the other. If we are failing to communicate, if we are arrogant or too self-deprecating, someone must tell us; are we reading the environment and other persons rationally?

We instruct one another by giving accurate responses and reactions to what is said and done. If we love persons we are forced in charity to tell them truthfully how we respond to them. Without this truthful response a person can continue in defensive self-deceptive traps. Often those who have been raised by too indulgent parents, or those in positions of great power who are surrounded by sycophants, or those who are greatly pitied or avoided, will not have the truth told to them. They do not get a proper education in self-knowledge because the human dialogue has been deficient or dishonest. Sooner or later they pay for the fact that others did not love them enough to tell them what they needed to know or to force them to confront the real consequences of what they do.

To instruct another in the struggle for self-knowledge is much like all instructing, a delicate task filled with paradox. One must tell the other when they are failing, while supporting and affirming them. It is no favor to mislead another out of mistaken efforts at nurturing. In this culture women have often been socialized to soothe, charm, lie, and cover up the faults of the men and children in their lives. Through timidity, mistaken kindness, or inattentiveness, many persons do not get in family life the instruction in self-discipline they need. The situation is far worse if a family is at the same time too ungenerous or meanspirited to affirm an individual's good qualities and potential strengths.

In many cases it takes psychological counseling to liberate and free the self from distorted past learning which no longer applies in the present. As in other instruction, the goal is to induce self-control and ongoing self-guidance. It is possible to learn to think about one's thinking and regularly examine how one feels and functions with other people. The more self-knowledge and self-awareness, the more freedom of choice. It is possible to learn to feel and act in new ways. Action, thought, and feeling can change if we make enough effort and have enough good and truthful companions to help us overcome our ignorance of ourselves. Self-control, or self-mastery, basically seems an ability to integrate consciously all of our different systems and levels of personality so that we can choose to act as we would.

Many of us who were educated in an earlier day were taught strategies of self-control in the family. Self-discipline was part of the Calvinist American heritage that fused stoic values and good manners. One was taught to cultivate cheerfulness and self-control as a contribution to the family and social circle; one should never be so self-indulgent or so rude as to litter the communal space with surliness or bad feeling. Ironically, psychological research has now vindicated the therapeutic value of many of the personal self-management strategies that parents and schools once taught. Stop pouting, don't dwell on your troubles, get busy, and you will feel better. Stand up straight, dress up, clean your room, and you will feel better. Go talk to others and you'll stop feeling self-conscious. Learn patience, finish what you start, and you'll feel better. Do something for others, be cheerful, and you'll feel better. Such strategies worked and still work; we can make ourselves feel better and change ourselves for the better through strategic efforts at self-control. What psychology calls self-management or self-control training, we called "character," the traits which you built through persistent effort.

Character means that individuals shape their environment, including their inner environment, as much as the environment shapes them. There is two-way influence. Freely willed effort can produce transformations of the unconscious and preconscious as well. Through effort, love, attention, and discipline those parts of the personality that seem beyond direction, awareness, and control can slowly be changed. Through consciousness and effort we can change much of our preconscious and emotional life. The method seems to be to deploy attention, the capacity which gives us freedom and makes self-management possible. Those parents, teachers, therapists, or religious guides who instruct us to know ourselves, and direct ourselves, and achieve disciplined self-control prepare us to be able to cope with life—and to be cheerful while doing so.

Many young people in our post-Calvinist culture do not seem prepared to struggle with difficulties. They have been so protected by loving parents and shielded by affluence that they are not ready for the tests of character and personal integration which life brings. The need for self-discipline, perseverance, and long-term effort is a surprise to them. That marriage takes sacrifice is a surprise; that one's work and career should take so much dedication and effort is easier to understand, but still something of a shock. The difficulty of balancing work and family becomes disconcerting if not overwhelming. And few are prepared for the struggles of parenthood in a time when much of the family and community support for child rearing has vanished. Today we see many young adults struggling to come to terms with adulthood, sadly ignorant of many psychological and spiritual truths that could help them.

RELIGIOUS INSTRUCTION

Religious instruction in our pluralistic secular culture is a form of missionary activity. While most of us would never go as missionaries to Africa or China or New Guinea, we can be faced with some of the same challenges of communication here at home. Surely followers of punk rock stars, the Cosmo girls, or materialistic yuppies can seem as foreign to many of us as any distant tribe. How do we convey the good news of the Gospel to people whose culture is such a variant form of our own that it is difficult for us to bridge the gap? Indeed, the world of our own children can be quite alien for many of us raised in the last gasp of the nineteenth-century ethic of honor, integrity, and self-discipline. It's a long way from the world of Lord Tennyson, Jane Austen, George Eliot, and Charles Dickens to videos of rock stars and game shows. Confronting the modern cult of instant gratification, with its accompaniment of anxiety, violence, pornography, and the trivialization of life, can be as difficult as a mission to head-hunting cannibals.

In our evangelizing efforts to overcome religious ignorance we will face all the age-old challenges of teaching and learning. The same paradoxes of all instructing apply. We must overcome the obstacles and resistance to change. We will succeed through empathy, love, attentiveness, and reliance upon the ever-present inner ally in others. The innate human thirst for truth, love, and contact with the Creator is present beneath all apathy and can be reached through hope, love, and perseverance. Yes, there will always be martyred missionaries, whether in the Amazonian jungles or the American slum, but the greater number of successes give evidence that all human persons can be moved.

All the usual strategies, hazards, and rewards of teaching operate in religious instruction. But there are a few different factors in religious instruction that Christians going forth to proclaim the good news of the Gospel should keep in mind.

Essential to successful religious instruction is belief in one's own message. Is my faith more than a notional, verbal business? Do I give my real assent with all my heart and practice what I preach? Only the doers of the word, not the idle chatterers about the word, make an impact. In all instruction one must to some degree exemplify what one would teach, but in Christian teaching this is the crux of the matter. If the core of the message is love and one does not love, the empty gong resounds with a deafening hollowness. If one is declaiming about truth and lives a lie, the hypocrisy invalidates the message. The medium is the message in Christian instruction. All efforts to instruct well will fail if the instructor does not seek inner integrity and a Christ-centered life. One must be good to be a good religious instructor.

Also important for good religious instruction is an understanding of what is essential to the faith and what is historically conditioned. I need to know what is necessary, central, and basic to the good news and what is peripheral, culture-bound, or even a matter of my individual preference. Many great masters of Christian spiritual life have repeatedly affirmed the necessary theological distinctions between the core beliefs of Christianity and the evolving, changing interpretations of the faith in different epochs. The contention is that if the center and the core is strong and deep, there can be a great deal of flexibility, variety, and change on the periphery. Philosophy of science has also distinguished between the central tenets of a theory or scientific paradigm and the ongoing flexible accommodations in less central corollaries as new evidence appears from experimentation and discovery. Within Christianity, the certain, strong, living core of the Gospel allows flexible change and accommodation as Christianity is actually practiced throughout the world; a universal living faith can change and be embodied in various ways.

When modern Catholic missionaries go to other countries today, they no longer attempt to export their own historically conditioned nineteenth-century American or European Catholicism to other cultures. Instead they give the essential seeds and try cooperatively to harvest the strengths of the people to whom they are sent and from whom they expect to learn. One missionary to the Masai people of Africa reports,

> After having explained God and Jesus Christ to the people I had come to the end of the good news. It might seem a bit abrupt but I believe it is true. After declaiming all that God has done in the world because of his love for the world and for human beings, and after announcing the depths to which this love has gone in the person and love of Jesus Christ, the missionary's job is complete. What else is there?

The people to whom the good news has been given then must become self-guiding in the Lord. They must build up a Christian community and a Christian practice that will sanctify their particular time and place. They alone can develop their specific incarnation of God's love.

The Christian missionary, like all instructors, wishes to become unnecessary. He or she aspires to pass on the essential framework and the processes which will produce a self-generating knowledge and wisdom. The point here is to introduce a new Christian to prayer, to Scripture, to the inner light of conscience, and to the ongoing Catholic Church, or body of Christ in which a Christian life can be lived. No one can be a Christian alone. Even the hermits or those Christians incarcerated in solitary cells under oppressive regimes were formed by their Christian communities and relied on their presence as a spiritual cloud of witnesses. In a solitary life the social world remains in the head and heart, for individuals continue to think and feel in those modes given by their formative community. For those not incarcerated, a real community is necessary so that one can show expressions of love. As early monks justifying the formation of communal monasteries put it, "If you live alone, whose feet will you wash?" We also need our Christian community to confirm the new social reality we construct by our common Christian belief, language, and action. Otherwise the world's reality reasserts itself, and our faith weakens.

Catholic Christians must have a community consisting of particular places and specific people—life is with people. The parish structure is one place where we find people and receive religious instruction. If the parish does not give much support, American Catholics can find many other supplementary Catholic communities in which to grow in the faith. America has from its inception been a society that understands the creative possibilities of free association, compacts, and cooperative groups. As a consequence, Catholics in America have many, many different Church groups in which to seek instruction, even beyond the formal Catholic educational system. Intellectuals have *Commonweal, Cross Currents, America*, various newspapers and theological journals, along with a multitude of guilds and professional groups. Those who are more activist and those who are more conservative have other kinds of societies and groups in which they can participate. Third orders and institutes of every kind exist. These volunteer associations of Christians can provide some of the framework and mutual instruction that persons need for their religious formation.

As in all efforts to know one's self, there is the constant struggle against self-deception. In religious life as in other contexts, only one's fellows can help one overcome this most intractable form of ignorance. We need our Christian community to correct our own biases and predilections. This is another reason why the individual's incorporation into an ongoing concrete historical institution is important. Everyone finds certain parts of the good news easier to accept than others. The self-deception that keeps us from seeing our own faults may keep us from accepting the fullness of the Gospel. The community corrects and complements selective perceptions; no individual alone can know it all and have the definitive last word with the Word of God.

Being in the Church also instructs us in humility and irony. There are always models before us who are far ahead of us in spiritual wisdom and virtue. They instruct by their example; sometimes their entire existence is instructive. The fact that great mystics, saints, theologians, and thinkers are in the community inspires us. The knowledge that other quite ordinary persons around us are living the Gospel more fully and heroically than we are gives perspective and balance. A nice irony emerges when the large view is achieved and Christians no longer take themselves too seriously. Humble detachment, gratitude, and the catholic long-term communal perspective encourages saving wit and humor. We instruct when we are merry and full of joy, graciously humble and happy in the teeming company of fellow pilgrims. Saint Paul understood this and urged Christian apostles always to use tact and wit and to instruct others with respect and gentleness.

Christian religious instruction stresses over and over again that the loving heart is the heart of the matter. All of us need constantly to be reminded that God loves us more than we could ever love, that God has gone before us, waits for us, and is constantly eager to respond to us. We can always lift our heart to God and seek the Lord within. The divine presence within, the inner light, is intensified after baptism and entrance into the community. Since the Spirit guides an individual from within as well as through the Church, a delicate balance always has to be achieved between a reverence for individual conscience and the authority of the Church. A Christian should feel supported by the authority of the communal faith, as well as enjoying the liberty of the child of God to find his or her unique way to God. The point was tellingly made by a priest who, preaching on Saint Ignatius's arduous life, said, "And this, dear friends was Saint Ignatius's way to God. Thank God it is not the only way." There may be only one entrance, but an infinite number of paths lead us to the gate.

Whatever our spiritual path, we must learn how to read the signals of the generic self-guidance called conscience. This spiritual self-evaluation process has been called the discernment of spirits and bears a family resemblance to the inner scrutiny of psychotherapy. Such discernment involves looking into one's consciousness, emotions, moods, thoughts, images, and attitudes and trying to understand them in the light of faith. It is a way to know one's self and respond to God through the self-knowledge, another effort to overcome the snares of self-deception and defensive blind spots. Our family, friends, religious community, and spiritual mentors can help with their good counsel, but each unique individual must make his or her moral and religious decisions. We have to seek our unique and special road. What does God will of me?

An old constricted, deformed misunderstanding of Christianity discerned God's will in whatever hurt most, was most difficult or distasteful, or entailed the most sacrificial suffering. This approach now is seen as a defamation of the gentle but liberating yoke of Christ. The greatest spiritual masters, including Ignatius, understand that God leads us through happiness, desire, and inclination. Happiness and joy are signs of the Spirit. Christ promises joy, peace, rest, and the abundant life; the positive emotions are a positive sign that we are progressing in the way of truth for us.

Of course if we have persisted in grievous sin or become addicted or have long been in a dissolute or downward spiral in our moral life, it may be that a change of course will be painful and difficult. Desire and pleasure may not be a reliable guide when we are running away from God. But even in such cases the pain of our repentance will produce a deeper more peaceful quality of joy than the rather frenzied manic pleasure of dissipation. Baron von Hügel, a great master of spiritual counsel, told those he instructed to differentiate excitement from zest. He felt that while zest was good, excitement was negative. We have known the excitement that comes from anger or from the lust for revenge or self-glorification. The evil excitements of lust seem to exist in many more forms than carnal desire. What Shakespeare wrote of "lust in action" is true: it is

> the expense of spirit in a waste of shame . . .
> Mad in pursuit, and in possession so;
> Had, having, and in quest to have, extreme;
> A bliss in proof, and proved, a very woe,
> Before, a joy proposed; behind, a dream.

Such mad feelings of shameful excitement are usually a sign to ourselves that what we contemplate is not good. Lustful excitement is also intrusive, obsessive, accompanied by contradictory disordered thinking and distortions of reality.

Zest, on the other hand, is a positive desire that gives us joy and happiness. We have zest when we feel most completely ourselves, most completely in touch with reality. Zest seems to be a form of passionate love and joy which is not a dream, not shameful, not an expense of spirit. Instead of leaving us wasted and exhausted, zest inspirits us and makes us soar and mount up with wings to our own greatest heights. We are high, but not fearing a fall. We have experienced these high peak feelings—when lawfully in love, when working in white-hot creativity, when worshipping, or when playing well. We may be burning, but with a fire of love's peaceful and happy flame.

Zestful feelings of desire and happiness are a signal to us from ourselves that what we are doing is good for us. God leads us by happiness to know what we should be doing. We become more truly God's work of art when we are becoming uniquely our selves, growing in heart and mind. In the discernment of spirits our positive emotions affirm the truer deeper self that we want to become, the person we want to be with our friends and family as well as when we stand before

God and the joyful company of the saints. Indeed, one criterion to use in appraising our present emotions, desires, and decisions is whether we think that the spiritual cloud of witnesses who surround us would approve and be glad.

Pain, anxiety, and depression will generally show us that we are on the wrong course for growth. Our negative emotions, like the positive ones, are signals arising from our emotional selves, our past experiences; they also should be taken seriously as psychological and spiritual indicators that must be evaluated. Often we can see ourselves regressing into the negative patterns of infantile thoughts and emotions that are quite destructive to our spiritual and psychological health. We can sense that our feelings of rage, despair, hate, jealousy, and selfishness are hardening our heart toward others. These feelings are experienced and directly discerned as not being fruits of the Spirit. Like lustful excitement, evil desires and fears are obsessive, intrusive, agitating, and make us conflicted and unhappy. We can feel our negative emotions drawing us toward serious sin.

The destructive power of the negative emotions, particularly of lustful excitement, has led many religious counselors and moral instructors, influenced by the stoic ideal, to recommend the overcoming of all emotion as the way to truth and perfection. The suppression of affection, particular attachments, and desire was seen as the way to freedom and self-mastery. Religious instruction and moral instruction included exercises aimed at curbing one's feelings, which were deemed either dangerous or irrelevant. A detached and completely rational approach was championed as the way the person should make all decisions. Along with the stoic philosopher, the detached and rational scientist was held up as the epitome of the nonemotional approach. Today, of course, the philosophers and historians of science have discovered that many factors other than rational deduction guide the scientific enterprise. We hear talk in science of personal and tacit knowl-

edge, intuition, belief systems, and faithful attachment to
theories, mentors and scientific communities. Science progresses by much more than exclusively rational and cognitive
methods of thought.

In religious and moral instruction emotions need to be
taken into account much more than has been the case. The
importance of reaching both heart and mind has to be stressed
in all instruction, and particularly in religious instruction.
Heart speaks to heart, said Cardinal Newman. It also turns
out that mind speaks to heart, heart speaks to mind, and mind
speaks to mind. The dynamic interplay between our emotions
and our thought, both within the self and with others, is being
newly recognized as a complex ongoing process that affects all
of our life. Sometimes thinking and reason should control and
constrain emotion, especially negative emotions. Negative
emotions such as despair or lust should not carry the day. But
at the same time positive emotions and heartfelt feelings can
tutor the reason.

Neither heart or mind can be discounted in instructing
other persons or in self-guidance. Therapists have had to face
this truth in psychological instruction and good teachers have
always known it intuitively. Now religious instructors have to
rethink their approach to educating the heart as well as the
mind. We need to revive the practice of the discernment of
spirits and meditate on the power of love to tutor the reason.
Love make us attend more closely, gives empathetic understanding, and inspires hope and perseverance. Our attachment, attentiveness, and desire give us creative insight into
the truth. Religious instruction has a new world to explore as
we mine the rich tradition of spiritual counsel and move
toward the new synthesis necessary in our psychological
times.

To instruct another is to collaborate with God, the One who
teaches and enlightens. There will be effort, pain, and joy in
this spiritual work of mercy, but love impels us to seek truth

and share what we have with others. Our God, who came to teach us personally and who instructs us from within, enkindles the fire to know and to teach in all hearts. We imitate the most loving, patient, and attentive of all teachers when we instruct the ignorant.

3

TO COUNSEL THE DOUBTFUL

When there are some who have doubts, reassure them; when there are some to be saved from the fire, pull them out. (Jude 1:23)

Simply reverence the Lord Christ in your hearts, and always have your answer ready for people who ask you the reason for the hope that you all have. But give it with courtesy and respect and with a clear conscience. (I Peter 3:15)

DOUBT

"I believe. Lord, help my unbelief." So said the centurion in the Gospels and so say we all. The first thing to recognize in counseling the doubtful is that everyone pursuing a life of faith will doubt. How could it be otherwise? Our faith is hope in things unseen. If matters were clear and evident there would be no need for faith. Faith implies a gap between what is fairly certain and what is only probable. We live in the realm of probabilities because we are not yet face to face with God, the ultimate reality.

Jesus, too, seems to have experienced doubt. The resounding cry of agony comes down to us across the ages: "My God, my God, why have you forsaken me?" Enough faith and assurance remain so that Jesus uses the words of the Psalmist to cry to the loving One who hears and cares for a son's pain, but the troubled "Why?" "Why so forsaken?" bespeaks doubt and uncertainty. If the Christ has not been spared such a troubling of spirit, then it is not surprising that we also will experience our intermittent doubts in the midst of belief, before and after belief, side by side with a sense of assurance and faith. Even faced with the resurrected Jesus, many of us, more skeptical than Thomas, would still doubt, in the midst of joy; we would think him an apparition too good to be true—we would say we might be dreaming, or perhaps experiencing a hallucinatory projection of our unconscious desires for a magic helper. The varieties of doubt, like the forms of faith and devotion, come clothed in the intellectual fabric of the day.

Faith always and everywhere is based upon the logical and psychological understanding that alternative readings of reality are possible. Faith and doubt are intertwined. However, there exists some decisive element in faith, some uncoerced personal assent of the whole person is involved, which tips the balance against inner doubt. As in a gestalt figure which can be seen as either vase or two profiles, faith emerges from the ground of doubt and dominates our perception of the whole picture. In this sense, the assent of faith is an activity, an active cooperation of perception with God's grace.

I think of the life of faith using the ancient imagery of light and darkness. Faith is a personal turning and stretching toward the sun; it is my part to open my eyes and let myself be drawn out of the dark corner where I huddle in misery. But choosing life, following the light to the sun out of the addictive land of gloom, is surprisingly difficult. To be doubtful is "to hesitate in belief, to admit of doubt, not to be clear or inclined not to believe." It is the inclination not to believe that creates the worst obstacle; there's something in us, profound inertia, that wants to subsist in darkness, taking some miserable pride in the finality of death and despair.

COUNSELING THE DOUBTFUL

Since all who believe must encounter doubt, counseling the doubtful can never be a one-way dispensing of the bounty of one's abundant faith to those without. Counseling in all its forms is much better understood as consultation or mutual deliberation, a coming together of persons with a common focus. Counsel can be taken in many ways. One can take counsel with one's self, reasoning and reflecting upon all of the different motivations and considerations within the complex personality we recognize ourselves to be. We can also take counsel with God within and without, through prayer and reflection, opening ourselves in silence and meditation. And we take counsel with other persons, meeting, discussing, reflecting, mutually considering some question or situation. As usual, the self-self interactions within, and the interaction with God, reflect our interactions with other persons, and vice versa. Those who never listen to others rarely look within. Closing off one's access to self and others will result in a closing off to God as well. Giving up on God engenders a despair that impedes reaching others. Certainly no one can counsel the doubtful who has lost touch with his or her own doubts and inner struggles, or who has lost the ability to ask for help from others. Even Jesus asked his disciples to watch with him, to support him with their presence, during his last intense inner struggle of doubt and prayer.

Would-be counselors must share their moments of hesitation and doubt with each other and take counsel and comfort from the sharing. It would be dishonest to pretend—especially to ourselves—that we do not experience doubt. Sealing off and denying doubts is the worst of all defenses, for things that are sealed off from self-scrutiny tend to gather irrational energy and often burst forth in more destructive forms. But we are also called to share our moments of certitude, joy, and faith. Fortunately, one's periods of deep doubt are not often concurrent with those of one's fellow believers or others who may be seeking counsel. It is always unsettling to think that one may be the only believer some people know well enough to approach. Who else can they ask about God, or speak to about spiritual things?

To counsel the doubtful is a spiritual work of mercy, and like the other spiritual works, it is a form of active love and care. It takes energy and time. It cannot be palmed off on priests or relegated to trained pastoral counselors or psychologists. In the broadest sense, one can see that Scripture, liturgy, and all spiritual writing and sermons are forms of mutual counseling by Christians to meet doubt. But counseling the doubtful more specifically applies to face-to-face encounters, conversations, and dialogues with persons we meet every day. When we try to love others, we move to meet doubt by the effort to extend and share our inner selves.

Counseling encounters with another may be formal or informal, very brief or extended in time. Over a long life there may be conversations we hardly remember that nonetheless affected another person. One of life's most gratifying experiences is to hear years after the event that some now-forgotten word of encouragement made a profound difference in another's life. A bit of seed fell on fertile ground and bore abundant fruit. How marvelous to hope that in the final judgment there may be a few forgotten good deeds to lay alongside the mound of failures and omissions that remain so painfully etched in the memory! Such experiences of counsel given and received defend us against the most disturbing deepest doubt of all, the anxiety that we are ultimately isolated and totally helpless to succor one another. The first requirement for counseling the doubtful is to believe that we matter to one another, we can make a difference. If we believe we are members of one another, it is worth the effort to try to connect. We must see each other through.

It seems clear that when we connect, we connect in many ways, and on many levels at once. Our words, nonverbal signals, silences, emotional messages, and deeds are all parts of communication. If counseling is the meeting of persons, all of these dimensions of a person-to-person encounter become important. Perhaps the most effective way to counsel a person who is hesitating in belief is to hold up the exemplary life of a believer or community of believers. Paul does this over and over in the New Testament. Would your doubts be persuaded? Look to your experience of faithful persons. By their fruits you shall know them. It does not take a philosophical pragmatist to understand the power of observing what works and what doesn't in spiritual matters. We test for soundness. Are persons acting on their beliefs? If they are Christians, do they love one another? Are they increasing in joy, peace, truth, good sense, prudence, good works?

The other day I was watching a film on Mother Theresa. She was confronting a group of secular officials in a struggle to enter Beirut to rescue some retarded children. I was impressed by the familiar cast of her efforts to persuade the doubting officials of her mission: "Come and see," she said. It is the ultimate Christian counsel to the doubtful. As Jesus sent an account of his liberating actions to assuage the doubts of John the Baptist, so all Christians have known that they must be ready to testify with their lives. Come and see if you would believe. Since counsel, or mutual meeting, takes place on all levels and through all modes of communication, dishonest signals and false claims become apparent. While many might disagree with Mother Theresa's approach to solving problems, few can doubt the sincerity and power of her belief in active love. Young women flock to her uncompromising order, devoting themselves to lives of hardship and service.

But Mother Theresa's community also understands that prayer and worship are necessary to keep their beliefs strong enough to continue the active practice of charity. Doubt is inevitable. A person cannot see Christ in the loathsome leper or repulsively deformed retardate unless one continues to find Christ in sacrament, Scripture, and prayer. Romantic gestures rapidly wither away without a stable source of spiritual power. The bottom line of secular wisdom asserts that human life is nasty, brutish, and short—we die like the animals and there is nothing after. Only communal worship empowers the Christocentric world view, which can overcome the doubts of the world.

If belief and knowledge are partially constructed and sustained by the social group, as sociologists of knowledge tell us, then one cannot be a believer alone. There must be others to confirm one's reality through consensual conversation. We who live in a pluralistic society, where the majority of people doubt and a minority believes, may never experience the certitude that we might have known in a time when every person shared basic assumptions and sustained each other's concept of the world. In contrast to the closed communities of the past, most of us today are forced to develop a more complicated way of believing to take account of doubt and disbelief. Counseling the doubtful and the need to be sustained by consensual conversation are both more necessary and more complex than they used to be.

But few would want to return to the parochial enclosed enclaves of an earlier day or another culture. Those narrow worlds exact their own price. Our struggles with our doubt and disbelief can produce spiritual growth, as they force us to become more complex self-conscious personalities. We can be humbly grateful that somehow through God's grace our faith is still stronger than our doubt. Gratitude helps us cultivate the saving irony and gracious detachment that keep us from taking ourselves so seriously that we become dogmatic, humorless, simpleminded and insufferable "true believers." How crude and offensive Christian fundamentalists and absolutists become. Experiencing an assault by a true believer can give a lasting lesson in how *not* to counsel the doubtful.

A woman acquaintance of mine, a divorced Hispanic lawyer and long-lapsed Catholic who was newly converted to a fundamentalist Christian group, once came to my house. Although I hardly knew her, she came on a mission to persuade me to declare myself for Christ. Thoroughly taken aback, I attempted to explain that I had been trying to be a faithful Christian for thirty years, since my own adult conversion. But she insisted that I must now profess with her my absolute certainty that I was saved and in communion with Jesus Christ, my savior. To help me overcome my doubts, she began to show me the relevant passages in Scripture (underlined by her pastor) so that I could announce my conversion and we could pray together.

A curiously embarrassing struggle ensued between us, paradigmatic of the clash between believer and true believer. I was filled with mixed emotions—simultaneously annoyed, touched by her fervor, and puzzled over what to do. I did not want to be rude or discourage her newfound faith, however aggressive, manic, and simpleminded it appeared to me. So I kept on protesting my own Christian faith and hope, while insisting that I was convinced that no one could ever be absolutely certain of one's salvation: hope, yes; assurance of God's love, yes; but *certainty*, no. I maintained that it was necessary in humility to recognize some doubt, since I was a sinful human being and God alone could be all-knowing. I feverishly quoted Saint Joan of Arc's great reply to the question of whether she was in a state of grace: "If I am, God keep me so; if I am not, may God speedily bring me to His salvation."

But my fired-up holy inquisitor dismissed my ideal of irony in the Christian life and my fear of presumption as mere waffling. She insisted and insisted that I could not be truly saved if I would not verbally profess my absolute certainty that I was saved. In the end I did pray with her and perhaps gave her some satisfaction and hope for my soul. At least I controlled my anger over her arrogant presumption toward me. She would barely listen to me. My faith and theology, not to mention my past writing or twenty years of pillar-of-the-parish efforts, were of no moment to her. I was simply a conversion opportunity in her newfound faith agenda. This basically comic experience at least made me seriously search my own conscience: Had I ever tried to steamroller others in the same way? Had I ever been as insensitive and imperious as this true believer?

The typical true believer, often met in fundamentalist cults and ideological movements, has violently suppressed all inner doubts and so has little trouble assaulting all dissent in others. After cutting off the inner dialogue, one can hardly communicate with other persons; only absolute submissiveness to the orthodox truth is acceptable. All inquiry or openness or dialogue is seen as dangerous since tight controls must be maintained at all times to suppress inner doubts. Even physically, true believers radiate tension and tightness in face and body (sometimes even tics and twitches) as they exert their defense of hypervigilance. The idea of using doubt to progress toward truth, or unbelief as a means to achieve humility and therapeutic irony is anathema to the closed mind. Nor is the human condition seen as comic; no merriment is allowed to deflect from the intensely serious struggle. Caught up in the cause, the person gains purpose and can avoid attending to the inner self or to personal problems. The true believer cannot counsel the doubtful effectively because the inner self must not be attended to; empathy for self and others fails. Self-doubt produces too much anxiety; all doubts must be displaced and projected and then countered by renewed assaults against outside enemies. The paranoid view of the world triumphs.

The great spiritual scholar and counselor Baron von Hügel wrote that some persons need to have their faith mapped out with geometric precision, with a clear and sharp boundary between belief and unbelief. He, however, espoused a more complex view. He saw himself as a person who possessed a strong center of faith and light, but he realized that as one moves toward the peripheries of faith there must be flexibility and a gradual indistinguishability of the boundaries between truth and untruth. He was a great spiritual counselor because he realized the many different ways to truth and could help individuals find the best way for them. Like all great counselors, teachers, therapists, or parents, his aim was to have the learner progress toward the ultimate goal of a mutual relationship of equals. Counselors, too, seek to be "biodegradable," to encourage the counselee to absorb what they have to give and pass it on.

As an intellectual, von Hügel also understood doubt; indeed, he recommended the pursuit of science, with its use of doubt and skepticism, as a corrective discipline for believers. (He also saw joy as a mark of the Spirit.) The case for complex irony in faith can be strengthened by remembering that Jesus himself did not claim to know or decide everything in absolute detail. He disclaimed knowledge of when the Last Day would occur and refused to be a judge in a case of brother against brother. He also refused to be called good: he knew what was in man as he knew himself. His authority and ability to counsel the doubtful contains no trace of arrogant assault, but is empowered instead by his love and acceptance of others.

When we are called to counsel the doubtful we must seek to know who it is we are meeting and value them. The ability to listen and truly learn how another sees the world is the first rule of any form of counseling. The famous rule that a counselor should tender the client unconditional positive regard and acceptance is really a secular translation of Christian charity. A true counselor will follow the lead of the Holy Spirit as Counselor. The Spirit is always working within us—suggesting, comforting, standing by us with love—in our journey through life. And if we wish to counsel others we have to make clear that we will stand by them whatever happens. Just as the love of Christ is the one thing we can depend upon, so anyone that we counsel should be able to depend unreservedly upon our love and understanding, our respect and empathy.

Each individual is a unique mystery unto herself or himself. While there are general laws and general orderings and developmental patterns in human personality, there is also something totally unique in each person. Christians believe that God has arranged it this way. Each person is made in the image of God; and God, who is infinite, is pleased to be imaged in multitudes of unique individuals—from the first human to the last—who can each be a part of the human creation in his or her own special way. In the last days, it is written, each person will receive from the Lord a white stone upon which a unique name known only to God and the self will be written. Obviously, unique persons, in their infinite variety, will believe and will struggle with doubt in many different ways. Explorations of the varieties of religious experience and belief can be matched by considerations of the differentiation of doubt.

William James is of course the classic and still reliable guide to the way different people experience belief and unbelief. He was one of the first of modern thinkers to point out that different personality types have characteristic religious experiences along with characteristic patterns of unbelief. James calls "healthy minded" those persons who believe easily and without effort; they tend to see beauty and goodness and joy and marvelous coincidences and confirmations of the good news everywhere. Evil and the darker side of life hardly exist for them; doubts do not often trouble them on their religious journey. These optimistic, happy, naturally mystic spirits are drawn to American religious movements of holistic health and Christian Science that deny the reality of evil. More pessimistic persons have great difficulty believing and overcoming their doubts; they will never rest easy in the face of the omnipresent evil and injustice they see in the world. Such tortured dark spirits find and sustain faith at great cost.

I think James is correct in his assessment of yet another set of persons who are more or less incapable of subjective religious experience. They do not believe, nor can they really be said to doubt. They are simply tone deaf to the spiritual dimension of the universe; religious questions seem meaningless. James attributes this spiritual color-blindness to innate temperament interacting with and abetted by particular cultural environments. Certainly the mid-twentieth-century dominance of a dogmatic secular humanism encouraged such persons. Faced with general working assumptions of atheism and agnosticism it has been easy for many persons to feel that religious questions are either regressive or neurotic.

I also think later psychologists following the lead of Jung are correct when they consider developmental life stages as relevant to religious experience. Personality type and individual uniqueness play large roles in faith and doubt, but so does the stage of the life cycle that a person is experiencing. Adolescence is a critical period for religious experience. Middle age and old age also force inner spiritual questions to the forefront of personal concern. Religious issues can be robustly suppressed as in youth, but the limits of life and the approach of death cannot be denied. Even after a life filled with great public and private fulfillment, with few betrayals or disillusionments, a spiritual restlessness of the heart can emerge. Oddly enough, those who have experienced the best that the world has to give are most susceptible to the vanity-of-vanities argument: How can it be that I have all of this, all of these good things, and it is still not enough? If the rich young man had been older, possessed of even more personal achievements, might not his encounter with Jesus have had a different outcome? At least his doubts would be different.

The loss of the rich young man whom Jesus grieved over, is a comforting reminder that Jesus understands that we, too, will often fail in our efforts to counsel the doubtful. The particular personality and stage of life, and the free choice of the other person, are as much factors in success or failure as our effort or level of skill. Our responsibility is to love, to care, to meet the other, to share our selves, and to do our best. In actuality we never really know what transpires in the inner spiritual journeys of even those we love and are close to. It is as delicate and mysterious a business as the comings and goings of the wind, for the Spirit bloweth where it listeth.

Henri Nouwen, one of our modern masters of the spiritual life, has remarked on how surprisingly difficult it is for believers, even religious professionals, to talk to each other about personal experiences of faith. Church politics, yes; faith experiences, no. In our culture we are much more likely to reveal our sexual lives and difficulties than we are to speak of spiritual difficulties or revelations. In some circles personal religious experience can become almost a taboo subject; only objective intellectual discourse is permitted. Are we reticent because we live in a time when the supernatural and the spiritual is denied, corrupted by television hucksters or horribly debased in various spiritualistic movements which are the staple of the tabloids? Andrew Greeley has said that in his investigations of religious believers he finds many, many people who have had spiritual experiences, but they do not tell those around them. A survey of the laity conducted by the Synod on the Laity also revealed surprising faith experiences never before revealed because "no one ever asked." Believers resist telling or talking because they fear the doubts of others and are afraid of being ridiculed or thought neurotic.

In our postpsychological age, of course, it is very difficult to achieve a balance of faith and skepticism. Our psychological knowledge of the tricks the mind can play on itself makes it difficult for us to trust spiritual experiences. We now know that persons can be deluded in their construction of meaning and in their sense of how things are related. We also know that we tend to notice what stands out in the perceptual field and ignore the background or the foundation. We tend to interpret everything that happens to us in certain biased ways. But it is also the case that we do not make up our stories out of nothing. There is evidence, there are facts, there are experiences that come in spite of other viewpoints and perspectives that we may take. Reality is partly constructed by us but there is also something out there that interacts with our constructions in convincing ways. As one secular scientist in a new area of mathematics has expressed it, the rationality of the universe has been imprinted in the human species throughout evolution. We have an innate ability to think logically and are fairly well adapted to making appropriate judgment.

Science in its most recent explosive developments has disclosed the universe in amazing ways. We have been forced to give up older pictures of a closed determined clockwork of cause and effect and confront natural mysteries concerning the open and dynamic nature of matter, time, space, and information. We know that we must function without the complete truth, while trusting in human processes of rational judgments, intuitions, and testing. In the open universe more things seem to exist than this world dreams of; but our business is to keep seeking truth and sorting things out as sensibly as we can. In common sense, as in science, we make our decisions about what to believe by looking at the big picture, the accumulated patterns of evidence, relatively weighing different explanations that we view against the rest of our life experience and personal knowledge.

The new philosophy of science demonstrates that no one in science can ever actually prove anything decisively by simple facts. Facts and evidence must be evaluated in the light of theories and basic assumptions. One is always working with tacit knowledge, communities of adherents, models, best interpretations, and the weight of probabilities. Paradigms can shift, new pictures emerge. The briefest excursions in the modern understanding of how science works is extraordinarily liberating (as von Hügel and Newman intuited) for the religious believer's understanding of what is involved in personal faith. The same complex processes of rational assent operate in common sense, science, and religious faith, although the supportive evidence differs. In religion, too, there are different ways of believing and doubting; the differences come from the qualities of the personal and reasoning processes that have gone into the outcome.

Many children and childlike adults believe in a way we would call superstitious because their beliefs are both irrational and immoral, having very little to do with the God we know as the Holy One who is Truth, Love, and the Creator of the universe. Usually, in the course of life, adolescent skepticism and rationality, in concert with religious education, will purify and refine the superstitious coarseness or sentimentality of childish immature faith. Finally, however, a mature faith culminates in what has been called "the second naiveté." While incorporating rationality and skepticism, one can also be mystical, experiential, and childlike in the good sense of what children bring to the faith. There is an acceptance of things beyond reason that are neither irrational nor immoral, things that cannot be empirically proven but that may be proven valid when tested by reason and by the good fruit they produce.

In the second naiveté, protected by the exercise of reason, one can go beyond reason and calmly accept what Blessed Cornelia Connelley called the fairy-tale elements of Christianity. We experience happy coincidences and answers to our prayers; unusual things happen that are difficult to explain in purely natural ways. I think it is important to accept these things, once called consolations or experiences of grace, without overrating them or underrating them. Though we cannot explain it, God's providence does seem to work through many small things and converging events in our lives. We don't dwell on these providential occurrences because we do not

wish to fall into superstition or the heresy of thinking that evil
and suffering are also sent by God. It is beyond our philosophical resources to figure out how God's love and care operate in
a universe that is assumed to be structured through random
chance events or laws of cause and effect.

We know that Creation is separate from God but sustained
by God, and we know that our will is free. Creation is basically
good but has somehow been made futile and is now groaning
along with us in the painful birth process of redemption. The
problem of explaining evil and unjust suffering while integrating into our faith the belief that "everything works together
for good" is beyond us. So although we cannot explain it, we
still have our experiences of comfort, answered prayers, heal-
ings, wonderful coincidences, little miracles, all of those little
flowers from Saint Teresa of Lisieux that reassure us that God's
providence and care is still operating. We continue with our
"peak experiences," our spiritual highs, our epiphanies when
God seems to be breaking through and coming to our rescue.
If we hold to our commitment to reason and the discipline of
rational inquiry, we can accept God's good gifts in gratitude.
Simplicity, too, is a gift.

If Christians in the mainstream were willing to share their
spiritual experiences more fully, they might help stem the
tide of superstition and false spiritualism that is rising in our
culture. The aridity and poverty of the secular establishment's
technological world view seems to be producing a backlash
against the rationality of the Enlightenment. A distorted affirmation of the spiritual dimension of reality fuels the spread of
astrology, cults, drugs, satanism, and the like. Such rever-
berations of the spiritual have always been with us and will
never be extinguished by secular materialism. When the dev-
ils have been swept from the house, something spiritually
potent and positive must take up residence to avoid the inva-
sion of a much worse set of demons. So it is all the more
important that Christians share the elements of their religious

experience that are magnetic enough to appeal to the imagination and love of people while they encourage sanity and health.

The issue of how much belief and doubt is appropriate came up at a recent dinner party of deeply committed Catholic intellectuals. The taboo against talking about private spiritual experiences was almost broken as we began to discuss our reactions to Marian apparitions and Marian devotion. Divisions emerged rather clearly. Some relegated the whole Marian thing to regressive superstition entwined with neurotic manifestations; since they themselves had always been left cold by Marian devotion this aspect of Catholic diversity was more or less meaningless, if not embarrassing. Another position taken by a sophisticated Jesuit was that it did not matter whether such appearances were true or not, but they were generally a good and positive thing to be valued in our religious tradition. My own argument, in this general mutual counseling of doubt, was that while I believed Mary could, would, and did appear to humankind, not all apparitions were authentic and it would be important to determine which ones were true and real and thereby valuable in our tradition. Neurotics and psychotics also have visions, and self-hypnotized power seekers, assisted by clever mentors, have been working the gullible crowds since the oracles of the ancient world. Every Marian appearance has to be tested by the complicated ways we judge the genuineness of all other claims and theories, religious or secular. We must constantly make efforts to distinguish various levels of probability and then give different levels of assent. Something may be possible, but it might not be probable or productive, given everything else we know about God, Mary, and reality. After the most cursory appraisal, I would judge the Marian appearances at Guadalupe as much more probable than the highly suspicious apparitions claimed in Queens, New York, with the Yugoslavian appearances somewhere in between.

My attitude toward Marian devotion has evolved from complete Protestant rejection to warm endorsement. I have moved from the severely purist stance, verging on iconoclasm, to deep appreciation and grateful belief. For me it has been a journey through Christ to Mary. By this I mean that devotion to Mary has grown as I was able to accept my whole embodied self as a fellow creature in a good creation. Some melting of pride and self-sufficiency has been involved in this development, some willingness to cry for a mother's help in a simple way. I firmly believe with the mystics that God is our Mother and Christ is our Mother, but this belief seems to be strengthened by devotion to Mary as Mother. In our culture, women, too, have to struggle to appropriate the traditional "feminine" qualities within themselves; women have been taught to suspect and doubt as weakness their allegiance to love, nurturance, motherhood, and feminine bonding. Marian devotion defends us against the phallic fallacies of our culture: the glorification of aggression, autonomy, and competitive individual achievement. In the world of the bottom line we need to affirm again and again that the bottom line is love. Our Mother of Mercy and Good Counsel strengthens our hope, our sweetness, and our life, slowly leavening us with love so that we can be worthy of the promises of Christ.

SPECIFIC STRATEGIES IN COUNSELING
THE DOUBTFUL

Reconsidering Faith and Reason

Christianity consists of a historical institutional incarnated life, an intellectual cognitive understanding of the faith, and perhaps most important an emotional heartfelt affective assent to Christ as Lord. A full religious life must incorporate all of these dimensions but each can also be a realm of doubt. Often the emotional assent is lacking, sometimes the rational or intellectual understanding of the faith is more troubling, or the incarnated community and historical ongoing existence of the Church presents a problem. When counseling the doubtful it is important to understand what is the real difficulty and how the different dimensions may be interacting. One strategy that often works wonders is what I would call a lightening-of-the-load approach through education. Some persons have a false idea of what or how one must believe in order to be a Catholic. (They usually have misconceptions about the operation of scientific proofs as well.) Theological education is then in order and may solve many dilemmas. Educational programs aimed at correcting theological misconceptions have been very successful in reuniting lapsed Catholics with the Church.

In the post-Vatican-II Church there remain many people who think that they must believe every jot and tittle of the tradition with the same measure of assent. They were educated by teachers who were often Irish-American Catholics still under the sway of the Counter-Reformation and the modernist controversy. They think one must absolutely believe everything up to a clearcut boundary; and one step beyond the boundary is heresy. It is all or nothing, take the whole thing, relinquish all doubts, or out. Nothing ever changes, and nothing ever should change. Many rebellious ex-Catholics display a morbid nostalgia for the old authoritarian Church; they could not abide this Church, yet they wish to see it preserved in amber. But if seekers have doubts that come from an intellectual misunderstanding of what is necessary for belief, they can best be counseled through good theological instruction accompanied by a realistic psychology of the person.

Unfortunately, many pre-Vatican-II types are often trained in an outmoded psychology that cannot accommodate doubts or problems of conscience. In an older view of the person, people were divided into separated parts and faculties; this view overestimated the ability of the faculty of the will to direct the intellect. This psychology implies that one can perform acts of will in order to believe. Deciding to believe is thought to be possible. If one wants to enough, and makes enough effort of the will, one can overcome doubts and make one's self believe. Such thoughts seem to be behind the use of torture or penalties or threats against those whose beliefs are out of line. There is little understanding that a free assent of conscience wells up from an integrated whole person.

Vatican officials who demand that dissenting theologians reconsider and retract seem to be following the older psychology in concert with a conservative reading of Vatican II documents. They seem to believe that through acts of will a person can dissipate doubts or considered dissent. Other more mundane examples of the old view can appear in family life or community life. If members of the family or group stop believing or drop away or lapse from the faith, other members may demand belief, and blame the person who no longer believes. They are assuming by their blame that a person can will or force assent to the faith. This is obviously a much too simple approach to understanding how one believes, how one doubts, and how one ceases to believe.

The whole person believes and doubts and the whole person decides to assent. One cannot decide by an act of the disassociated will to override one's rational perception of what is or is not really the case. One can perform acts of love or hope or trust, but not decide to assent to reality contrary to one's considered opinion. Psychologically it is impossible to believe that what I believe to be so is not so. Yes, one can always reconsider and persons dedicated to seeking the truth must grant that subjectively they may be wrong, but in any final confrontation with oneself it is impossible knowingly to retract what one knows to be one's own view of reality at the present moment. If one happens to be in error or to be self-deceived, then by definition one cannot perceive it. After self-scrutiny and all-out efforts to seek the truth, one can only believe what one believes. God, who is a God of truth and honesty as well as love, will understand an honest person's inability to lie about what he or she truly perceives to be reality.

An impasse of faith should not be countered by counseling a doubting person to make some sort of absurd leap of faith or enter into the calculating wager on God's existence that Pascal recommended. These solutions seem either too irrational or too coldly rationalistic. To recommend irrational leaps of faith, to glory in the absurd, implies that reason and truth are not part of the divine plan, and that God does not want us to think as well as we can. Faith must be an assent beyond reason, but it is a reasonable and probable, never an irrational or absurd, step. We can reason to the point where we know that it is reasonable to hope for more than can be seen or proven, but our hope never rejects rationality or God's great gift of reason.

At the other extreme, Pascal's wager or calculation on the existence of God seems unsatisfactory in its rationalistic approach. Pascal recommends a cool cost-benefit analysis in which betting on God's existence ensures heaven, avoids hell, and produces a better human life even if death proves to be the end of human consciousness. Does this approach really overcome doubt? It seems offensive to the modern sensibility because of the impersonal, selfish calculation involved, and the implication that one can just decide to believe. Why would God be pleased by such a wager? We ourselves would not want a person to decide to marry us in order to avoid harmful consequences, or through a calculating gamble on the goods we could bestow. The motivation for taking up the wager would corrode the whole relationship. Honest doubt seems preferable to us. Besides, if anyone ever actually employed Pascal's wager it was probably because they already believed in some vague way, and lived in a culture where most people believed. In any case, it seems psychologically impossible to force mental assent *de novo* by an act of will.

A God who has put the light of reason in our minds and written an inner law of love upon our hearts would not want human beings either to deny their reason or to come to faith through force or calculation. We glorify God as the God of truth and the source of all knowledge by seeking truth, the whole truth, and nothing but the truth. Our part is to seek, to open readily our eyes and ears, to wait, to respond, and never to harden our hearts; but at the same time we must never coerce or lie to ourselves about what we think or feel. The gift of faith is a reasonable extension of the light of reason into the light of loving assent. God draws us on through the best that is in us. Someone once described religions as being not science-minus but poetry-plus. This is not adequate because religious belief is science-plus as well as poetry-plus, and love above all. I do not think one should counsel the doubtful by asking for existential wagers or leaps into absurdity. Other counsels, other strategies, and more holistic approaches to doubt can be explored.

Patience and Perseverance

Patience and perseverance are an old tried and true strategy for dealing with doubts and periods of troubled belief. Most of us never progress to the advanced stages of spirituality that are described as the mystic's dark night of the soul, but almost everyone experiences times of unusual storm and stress, or times of extreme emptiness. How should one deal with such periods when they occur in a life of fairly solid belief? The old answer is, "Wait, it will pass," and continue with business as usual. The approach of patience and perseverance is like taking shelter and waiting for the storm to pass. After all, anyone who has lived very long, or at least passed through adolescence, knows that life can sometimes resemble a roller coaster of inner and outer ups and downs. Moods and emotions may move from highs of exultation, well-being, and near ecstasy to lows of total depression and despair. Many volatile yet normal temperaments suffer such shifts of mood very rapidly. Other persons may go beyond the normal range of ups and downs and suffer the exaggerated violent mood swings of mental illness.

It is difficult to differentiate the normal from the abnormal, but extreme depression or extreme mania become so out of touch with common-sense reality that they manifest the need for professional treatment. But persons well within the range of normal still must deal with the mystery of change in daily consciousness and function. In one's psychological life, and in the life of faith, there can be cycles similar to those experienced by athletes. One may experience "hot" periods, when everything clicks, alternating with grim losing streaks, when nothing works and one is hardly in the game. Psychologists are busily researching the way we unconsciously and pre-consciously process external and internal stimuli, so perhaps we shall someday understand more clearly the natural causes behind our ups and downs, or why certain ideas or feelings seem to pop into our minds. Freud's insights into the unconscious are being submitted to rigorous experimental investigation. However since by definition we cannot be aware of our unconscious, we are still left with the problem of how to cope. Given the oddity and complexity of our minds, it is no wonder that persons have always been willing to blame evil thoughts and temptations on the Devil or demons.

Whatever their origin, a multitude of manic, depressive, doubtful, and depraved notions can beset very normal persons; such notions appear as out of nowhere in the ever moving stream of personal consciousness. Maybe I am an omnipotent god in disguise who can heal, or fly, or control all things; surely I exist beyond all good and evil. Or again, life is absolutely meaningless, ultimately unbearable, so I will kill myself. Or, I'll take revenge on my enemies and torture them slowly, or kill this innocent person for no reason. Or, I'll run away from home, family, work, and duty. Such dreadful momentary impulses come to many a mind, but the point is that in normal functioning they are jumbled in with a thousand other neutral and loving thoughts, and they disappear as quickly as they come. Our sense of reality and moral commitment dissipates our weird impulses. All we need do is wait a moment and we come to ourselves.

So, too, moments of doubt arise and pass away. In the approach of patience and perseverance, one does not panic, seek to repress doubtful thoughts, or fight back. Knowing the law of least effort, one does not become engaged with or focused upon evil or doubt by struggling with it head on in mortal combat. A better strategy is simply to quiet oneself, fully recognize the doubts as they emerge, and calmly wait. When the bedouin riding his camel meets the overwhelming sandstorm in the desert, he stops, gets off, lies down in the sand, covers his head, and quietly waits for the storm to be over. Storms do pass and doubts disappear. A wise person does not dissipate energy in a struggle when time alone will take care of a problem.

Another strategy is to continue calmly going about whatever it is that has been the subject of doubt—one's worship, prayer, job, marital life. When the storm passes it becomes clear that this was what one should have been doing. Belief returns. To keep on keeping on, to persevere, renews hope and strengthens our commitments. Fidelity deepens the bond. When we persevere through difficulties we give testimony to the fact that we trust and identify with our former self and our own past goals, roles, promises, and commitments. We learn to increase our trust and respect the self that brings us through the problematic or conflicted periods of doubt. We trust our self, the person who made those earlier decisions, enough so that we do not overturn the commitments we decided upon in an earlier time.

The human ability to make promises and commitments and to adhere to principles is based on our psychological understanding of the fluctuation and complex multiplicity of personal consciousness through time. We know that superficial inclinations, passing desires, or other vicissitudes may tempt us to give up or change purposes. So we bind ourselves for the future, staking our self-respect. When we make a promise we affirm that we can now know what we should do in the future no matter what may happen and, even more confidently, we affirm that we will be able to direct ourselves and carry through in the face of all inner and outer countervailing forces. It takes self-esteem and self-confidence to engage in commitments for the future. Self-esteem and self-confidence in one's past produces perseverance despite difficulties and doubt.

But this process of perseverance and fidelity is not a simple opposition of reason and emotion in which reason must conquer desire or emotion overcome reason. The challenge during periods of doubt can come from any dimension of my self: I might meet new intellectual problems or feel new desires. It will be best for me if the promise or past commitment or personal principle to which I now adhere emanated from an action of an integrated self. Principles, too, are not merely abstract moral rules, but can be seen as a form of crystallized, self-appropriated, chosen emotions. The principle, say, of justice embodies the best empathetic emotions I have felt; these crystallized emotions condensed into the principle will serve as a bridge over those times when I am assaulted by less welcome emotions or less admirable attitudes. I can persevere through periods of doubt because I have experienced more certain feelings in the past and remember my allegiance to these better, stronger, truer, feelings. My heart can serve to keep me true to myself.

Strategies of Heart and Deed

Suppose we have hardened our hearts in doubt. Is there an acceptable strategy for counseling doubt that directly affects our emotions and thereby counters doubt? Are there actions to be taken that can strengthen the inner self's progress toward faith? Ancient spiritual wisdom has always pointed to the effectiveness of certain practices of penance and self-purification, and the effort to change the desires of the heart through cultivating detachment or through new attachments. One seeks to purify and dispose oneself for higher and more encompassing attachments; the effort is to try to detach oneself from anything that may cloud the truth or get in the way of progress. What in my life now impedes my desire to move toward God's love and truth? What may be getting in the way of someone who comes to take counsel with me?

Spiritual seekers from time immemorial have testified to the fact that changing and simplifying certain parts of life help a person to open up and see things more clearly in other parts of their lives. Traditionally the demand was made for poverty, chastity, and obedience as the great simplifiers and major requirements for spiritual progress. Today, for the laity or those engaged in the world, the required moves may be less clearcut and more subtle. In most vocations persons must spiritually progress through the affirmation of the world and through loving commitments to spouse and family. This means there is a need to strengthen our deepest desires for greater commitment amid the distractions of irrelevant trivialities.

Each of us must ask, What do I really want from God? To make progress or cure doubts we may have to give up certain kinds of slothful pastimes that draw us into things which we do not really want to be doing. Certain social circles—or habits, such as endless consuming or procrastination—may make our inner and outer environment cluttered and confusing. Will I see more clearly if I give up alcohol or drugs that I imbibe in nondamaging amounts but that still serve as a screen from self-consciousness? Do I need more time for retreats, or do I need the sustained self-examination of therapy? The goal is not to overcontrol or do violence to the self but to use discipline to get in better psychological shape. Ascetic practices must serve the purpose of clearing the ground, making it more open to receive and give love.

Performing acts of love and hope also seems to be within the realm of will. One often has emotions that arise and overwhelm us in an uncontrollable way, but at other times we can control or deflect feelings through an inner conversation with ourselves or through willed deployments of attention. We can control attention and attention controls emotive feelings to a great extent. We are often able to initiate acts of love and affection, and to desire the good of others. Love begets more love. To love and to encourage and feed the fire of our love of God and humankind seems to help resolve our intellectual difficulties. Love helps the mind penetrate problems because with empathetic feelings of love we concentrate on the desired object, we pay attention and find it easy to persevere in efforts to understand. When we care, we will continue to wrestle with doubts without giving up.

The need to enlarge our hearts in the struggle with doubt is also behind the strategy of seeking counsel from those that we love and admire. We pay heartfelt attention to those whom we love and judge to be good. God usually leads us through persons. We learn from others by loving them and seeking to understand that which they love. The good and the wise person who is a loving person helps us resolve doubt because we try to perceive as they perceive; we also want to acquire whatever personal qualities they exhibit. The great souls who love much, inspire love and faith in others. Through the power of love persons are led from doubt to affirmation and to belief. A community of persons who inspire love and admiration is the most potent therapy for doubt.

On the road to Emmaus we have an example of Jesus counseling the doubtful. Jesus instructs the troubled disciples discouraged by the debacle of the crucifixion and the crash of their hopes for change. In an intellectual exchange he interprets and elucidates the Scriptures for them; he uses verbal cognitive instruction to make sense of their present situation. But he also reaches out to them in an affective way and induces such love that they press him to stay on with them. When he acts by breaking the bread and eating, the Lord is recognized fully. Of course, they say, did not our hearts burn within us when he counseled us? The power of intellect, love, and the communal act transform doubt into belief.

Newman, an acute philosopher of faith, spoke of differentiating a notional assent from a real assent to truth; the difference seems to be that when the affective and emotional capacity is fully integrated with the cognitive intellectual capacity, real assent occurs. As psychologists well know, without emotion and feeling integrated with an intellectual or verbal understanding, nothing is fully understood or grasped. Dissociated or verbal accounts or notional explanations can be given and make rational sense, but without the appropriate feelings, real understanding is missing. Psychopaths can verbally explain the moral rules, but they do not feel the moral emotions of guilt or empathy that produce moral behavior. A bereaved person can verbally describe a loss, but cannot really take it in until the appropriate emotions have been felt. So, too, we can intellectually explain doubts but we cannot really, deeply believe or be able to counsel another if we cut off emotion. Heart speaks to heart; the heart ensures good counsel.

FAILURE AND LIVING WITH CHRONIC DOUBT

Since our hearts are involved in efforts to counsel the doubtful, our failures inevitably produce pain. Jesus felt sad when the rich young man turned away; he was heartbroken by personal betrayal and rejection. The old-fashioned devotion to the sacred heart of Jesus acknowledges the importance of human emotions and the heartbreak that occurs when we fail to reach those we most love and care about. Often every effort to counsel the doubt of those most dear to us has been confounded. They do not respond. We must live with members of our families and with good friends who are alienated, doubting, and separated from the Church. In the old days leaving the Church was so traumatic that it was not as common as it is today. Now most families, and certainly all circles of friends, are full of those who are lapsed Catholics or Catholics by convention only. We live among chronic cases of doubt. After all our efforts have failed, how do we continue on?

Certainly we should never become defensive and separate ourselves from these doubtful persons that we love and hold in friendship. We have to avoid taking on the guise of true believers, complete with their angry and paranoid style. ("How dare you continue to doubt when I have given you my best conversion efforts? A plague on you, faithless one.!") Instead, we must stay calm and loving, continuing to talk about our own doubts and difficulties, never pretending that we are always full of certainty and assurance in order to set a good example. Being open about our own weaknesses and problems of our faith, being ironic and humorous about our faith, can keep us in touch with our own doubt and in touch with the doubtful. They must know that they are not that different from us in our own waverings and our own struggles.

But in the same way we should share our wonderful moments of certainty and happiness and joy when we feel that

God has been particularly good to us. Sometimes out of a kind of overdelicacy and discretion, believers who live with the chronically doubtful don't share their triumphs and happinesses in the faith, out of fear that it will look as though they are proselytizing or condescending to the other. A simpler, less self-conscious approach achieves a better balance. So maybe we have struggled over these questions in the past, but now I'm just going along and telling it like it is today, since this is too large a part of my life to keep in the closet.

But my openness and honesty must be above suspicion—even in my own mind. I should never be secretly plotting or calculating to convert or influence others. This kind of covert apostleship, often recommended by certain groups, such as Opus Dei, who talk of the apostleship of the luncheon table, seems repugnant in its deviousness. Christianity should be open, it should and must be transparent, liberating, and free. Needless to say, the secret manipulation of others through playing upon their irrational fears or desires is not true to God's example of loving friendship.

An attitude of respect and openness, for self and other, comes from a reverence for the varieties of individual spiritual journeys. God deals with everyone in unique ways and each person is different. What works for us and may be our way may not be the way of another. Convinced of our own uniqueness and trusting that God will help us through all our ups and downs, we can also let go, and trust that others will find their way. They are probably living as well as they can, hardly welcoming the doubt or the condition that they find themselves in. If they ever seek us out again for specific counsel, we are, of course, ready, but we don't push, coerce, or judge them to be inferior.

We can hope that those who doubt may someday believe, but our hope must spring from our perseverance in our own faith. Our main business is to live a life that day by ordinary day will witness to what we believe. Saint Paul talked about wives who sanctified and saved their husbands by their loving life in God. Parents, children, spouses, brothers, sisters, and friends can also hope that by their own perseverance and effort, their struggle to grow in love may help the beloved others who share one's life. Love overcomes all things, and God has eternity to work with. God wins, but we may not live to see it.

If and when we do see the doubtful ones return to strengthened faith, we are gloriously grateful and glad. The parable of the lost sheep is also psychologically true. But sometimes we have to be modestly, quietly, tactfully glad. We would not want to make certain sensitive prodigal sons feel guilty or bad or inferior to those who were more steadfast. We may consider steadfastness to be the most important of all virtues, the most needful thing for the service of God. But it is only through the grace of God that the steadfast stand, and continue to maintain their fidelity and equanimity. Of course if the prodigal son himself glories in the return and wishes to celebrate, then the feast can be readily joined. Such gladness is indeed a foretaste of the ultimate universal reconciliation we hope for in the marriage of the Lamb.

Doubts, trials, separations, and suffering test and prove our love. The best counsel we can give is to enlarge our hearts, seek God's wisdom, and live in the Spirit more completely. We, too, want to be able to say to the doubtful, come, come and see. God's power can transform us so that we, too, can give good counsel and our hearts pour forth living water.

4

TO COMFORT THE SORROWFUL

I will comfort you, as one is comforted by his mother. (Isaiah 66:33)

You now have sorrow; but I will see you once again and your hearts shall rejoice, and no man shall take your joy from you. (John 16:22)

CONFRONTING SUFFERING AND SORROW

To think about suffering is always difficult. We hate to suffer so much that the very thought arouses anxiety. We know that we should comfort the sorrowful if we are going to be Christians who imitate God's love and mercy, and part of us wants to do so, but still we shrink from the effort. As one young woman put it, "I always want to run away when I have to go to see someone who has lost someone they love." The urge to run away from suffering is a very basic human response.

We are ambivalent toward the sorrowful. A primitive superstitious fear whispers that we, too, may be drawn into the other person's suffering and be dragged down with them. Suffering seems to pollute and contaminate those unlucky ones singled out for misfortune; if we avoid them and turn away our face, perhaps we can avoid their fate. Irrationally we tell ourselves that if we can deny the reality of suffering then it won't have power over us. If one never goes to funerals or visits the sick in hospitals, and resolutely stays away from those having breakdowns, bankruptcies, divorces, or other crises, one may be spared similar evils.

As Americans we have other problems with suffering—especially suffering that cannot be rectified immediately. If we can do something about a problem we will readily wade in and work to fix things. But when we come up against sorrows that cannot be alleviated, they induce anxiety in a can-do people who insist on transforming the world rather than accepting fate. Our very virtues of optimistic activity often handicap us in the giving of comfort. Of course there are also more realistic problems inhibiting us from comforting the sorrowful. How can one do it adequately? Is it possible to find meaning in suffering?

The question of why so much human suffering exists, remains an inescapable problem for all believers in a benevolent all-powerful God. This difficulty has obsessed religious thinkers, at least since the writing of the Book of Job. Job's comforters did not do a very good job, but their mistaken and unsatisfactory efforts to explain and justify Job's condition with easy explanations of evil are still being handed out to those who mourn. But in reality, no simple approach can clarify the problem of suffering because it comes to human beings in so many varieties and forms, arising from so many different causes. Today some Christians have the opposite problem of Job's comforters: in a charitable age stressing the power of the external environment many find themselves unable to admit that some suffering is justly deserved and brought on by freely chosen wrongful acts.

Some sorrows being endured by a person are the direct consequences of the individual's free choice of evil. At times people actually receive immediate commensurate punishment in this life for the morally wrong choices that they make. The punishment fits the crime. There are cases where a person trying to harm and destroy an innocent person, instead brings about his or her own downfall. The movie villain in a car chase tries to kill the hero and rams his own car over the cliff. More common is the case of a person who, after leading others to take dangerous illegal drugs, suffers an overdose. How should a Christian respond to cases of justly deserved suffering? Should comfort be offered? Unfortunately these cases of just and appropriate consequences make up only a minuscule portion of the world's suffering.

More often we confront situations in which people err and do bad things but the consequences are disproportionate to the evil intent. Utter disasters often follow relatively minor acts of wrongdoing. A pilot is culpably careless and a plane full of people crashes. Someone sets a fire in frustration and anger but the fire spreads through a whole neighborhood and kills twenty persons. Drunk driving or engaging in sex outside marriage often produce terrible consequences far more serious than the bad motivation involved. Certain behavior that the culture condones as romantic or daringly rebellious can set off chain reactions. The suffering that ensues is not totally undeserved, but is disproportionate to the lapse or wrong committed and also is visited upon innocent bystanders. Much personal neurotic suffering from pride or wrong desires or inflated narcissism also falls into this category.

There exists also the huge amount of human suffering endured by completely innocent persons in totally unjust and unfair circumstances. There is no rational justification or explanation for most of the human suffering that we see in our world. In our lifetime we have seen several genocides destroy millions of innocent people: the Armenians, the Jews, the victims at Hiroshima, the Cambodians. Human inventiveness and technological mastery of nature have made human beings able to compete in destructiveness with monumental natural disasters. Worse still, the combined use of psychology and technology makes possible new forms of cruel and inhuman brainwashing and torture practiced in prisons all over the world. Weapons, terrorism, and open warfare become ever more cruel. Every time Beirut explodes or India riots we see again the sufferings imposed upon innocent victims.

Nature also regularly turns against human life in droughts, earthquakes, floods, tornadoes, volcanic eruptions, poisonous gas clouds, and tidal waves. Evil seems to exist in every form. Disease, viral illness, and genetic deformity inflict unjust suffering everywhere. Innocent children suffer because of their parents' neglect and active abuse in new and horrible ways. A disease such as AIDS, for instance, is bad enough in adults, but even more dreadful in an innocent child who is born facing a horrible and undeserved fate. Human suffering can take every shape and form, from natural disasters to the suffering of infants to the self-conscious pyschological suffering of highly sensitive individuals who may commit suicide out of depression. Confronting the human condition, many persons have despaired. How can one confront evil and still comfort the sorrowful?

We must look more closely at the psychology of suffering and the actual experience of individual persons. In acute attacks of grief and suffering, no matter what the cause or what the situation, pain seems to flood into or infuse personal private consciousness. One can feel one's self-awareness sinking into a sea of pain, either being immersed or experiencing the suffering in repeated waves. Whatever the cause, organic or psychological, human suffering quickly becomes an amalgam of physical and psychological distress. Mind and body can become one in pain, confirming that we are embodied beings. Suffering suffuses the person with its reality with only small bastions of resistance remaining as islands of high ground in a sea of distress. Mental and physical pain is acutely real, if hard to describe, and seems to throw us into a different subjective dimension of conscious reality. One can barely remember the other mode of being when immersed in a state of painful consciousness.

The subjectivity and unique experiencing of pain is important to remember. Suffering from something that is objectively or rationally unimportant can still be acutely painful and overwhelming to the person undergoing it. Taking the subjective psychological point of view seriously is a first requirement for those who wish to comfort another. An adult, for instance, has to understand that the child who is suffering, or the adolescent, or the neurotic, who is suffering over some objectively small matter, can be suffering as deeply as the strong adult broken by deep and dreadful tragic circumstances.

Suffering is also differentiated by whether it is sudden, acute, or an ongoing chronic state. The duration is important, particularly if a person is still in a state of shock. Confronting the unexpected takes its own mental adjustment. How is the person making sense of what is happening? Anyone who wishes to comfort the sorrowful has to think about how the person is interpreting the sorrowful experience. Does it seem unjust or unfair? Is the suffering seen as something unique to this particular individual or a part of the common tragic heritage of human beings? Is this suffering something that can be seen as temporary, or an irreversible tragic loss?

A particular individual may have to face a chronic condition in which his or her creativity and gifts are permanently thwarted by circumstances. We can suffer knowing that we have missed opportunities and will never be able to be as competent and creative as we could have been. Missed social opportunities may also produce isolation and loneliness. Many women and minority group members have seen their best talents wasted, through no fault of their own. Sorrows, of course, can also arise from the realization of things that were our fault—misspent years, wasted opportunities, or wrongs done to others. The sorrow arising from guilt and contrition can be oppressive. We can be forgiven by God, but often it is too late to make things right with those we have hurt. The death of our loved ones, especially deaths by suicide, produce painful losses, but can also possess an admixture of guilt. The unfinished business that we may have with another who has died adds to the complexity of the sorrow.

Then there is the pain and suffering that we experience from being actively hurt by others. Psychological sorrows arising from interpersonal conflict can be just as devastating as any larger social misfortune, or natural disaster. There is pain when one is misunderstood, ignored, or unappreciated. Struggles with those one respects and admires or loves hurt terribly. Perhaps the worst psychological suffering comes from a personal betrayal or when one is falsely accused by a beloved person. I have often thought that the greatest suffering that Jesus must have experienced was that of being betrayed and falsely accused. The rejection by those who should have appreciated him most would have been far more painful than persecution by the foreign Roman oppressors.

Sorrows between friends or colleagues or marriage partners can also arise when there is conflict and a divergence of beliefs. Good marriages may include acute moments of suffering, while bad marriages specialize in the high regularity of lower-grade miseries; since the general expectations, satisfactions, and love given are greater in good marriages, the painful hurts that do arise are more intensely disappointing. We are always more hurt by those with whom we have more in common, as demonstrated regularly in interreligious struggles, civil wars, and family struggles. Parents and children can hurt each other almost as deeply as beloved marital partners.

We also experience vicarious suffering for those we love and like. Watching others make mistakes or undergo trials when we cannot help them produces pain. Mary's suffering at the cross can be understood by every parent as an enactment of the worst the world can offer: helplessly watching a beloved child be tortured to death. At another extreme, others we love can torture us when they reject and turn against our expectations and hopes for their moral flourishing. We can be truly disillusioned and distressed by the downfall of those we admire. The concept of collective honor, or being dishonored by our own kin or clan or country is not now in vogue, but there can be a real distress suffered when one feels ashamed of one's own. This kind of sorrow becomes even deeper when a trust or common cause is betrayed. A grave public sorrow and shame can be felt over the wrongs committed by one's country or religious community or some other group with which one identifies.

Some psychologists have interpreted such public political sorrows to be in reality a screen or cover for some unacknowledged personal difficulty. This reductionism seems thoroughly misguided. While it is true that some very neurotic or even psychotic persons can latch on to public causes and distant problems as manifestations of their own illness, normal idealistic persons can be genuinely distressed over communal failures. Psychologists such as William James and Gordon Allport realized that the self extends its boundaries to identify with other people or ideals, so that larger groups and causes become an extension of the self. Those who truly identify with their country, religious group, profession, or institution can suffer when that group does not live up to its own standards.

Certainly the prophets of Israel suffered over the lapses of the people. And members of the affluent first world often feel deep shame and sorrow over what our country does or neglects to do. Anyone who lived through the Vietnam War or the Christmas bombing of Cambodia can remember the gloom that spread in our private and collective lives. So, too, the assassinations and riots in the 1960s engendered a public sorrow that those who loved their country could not shrug off. Many today suffer anxiety and near despair over the global threat of nuclear destruction and our country's part in maintaining the danger. Such sorrows are real and not a projection or symptom of personal neurosis.

The catalogue of the different forms of suffering and sorrow that exist pose for Christians a challenge that is nearly overwhelming. If we are to comfort the sorrowful we must recognize the extent and depth and differences that exist in the call. After confronting the range of sorrows we must ask what exactly we mean by comfort.

COMFORT

If suffering makes us anxious, the idea of comfort makes us uncomfortable. We are often uneasy at the thought that there is any comfort to be had; it seems a denial of the seriousness and sorrow that we experience in life. Surely, the bad news is the real news, and to believe in comfort is to succumb to the various opiates of the people, the pie-in-the-sky-when-you-die denial of the reality of evil and injustice. Is not gloom the mark of serious grownup persons who accept the sad reality of the universe? If we fully accept the sorrow and suffering of the world we should look with a steely eye on all attempts to comfort ourselves and others. Sophisticated wordly circles seem to cultivate agnosticism and a staunch stoicism at their best; at their worst, the reigning spirit of the world is one of sour cynicism.

Are we not better called to afflict the comfortable, rather than to comfort the afflicted? Certain persons courageously attempt to be prophets in their time: they exude despair and convince others of the seriousness of their purpose by their unrelieved pessimism and heavy, heavy concerns over the hypocrisy and sin of the world. Occasionally, the gloom and doom seem assigned by gender. While males despair, females offer hope and reassurance. The illusionless man journeys with the visionary maid—a perennial parable. Undoubtedly, comfort is seen as feminine because our first comfort comes from mother. Indeed, a certain level of comfort and hopeful cheerfulness is a characteristic of maternal thinking and practical nurturance; if it were not, no child would survive to become an adult.

Thus, comfort and comforting inevitably take us back to earlier dependence upon our mothers and caretakers. The comfort of touch, the comfort of love given physically, the comfort of our pleasure-giving bodily processes of eating and sleeping, are effective, early learned ways of comforting ourselves and others in distress. The joy of interpersonal attunement and emotional accord is also experienced between mother and child. Such affirmations of one's whole self may be reexperienced in adulthood in loving sexual intercourse. Sex is a comfort when all the different levels of personal being are engaged and give life to happiness. To love and be loved, with or without sexual expression, is the greatest comfort known to human beings. To be loved by those who are known and familiar, to be loved by one's own, adds to the comfort and joy. Familiar persons, routines, and places can affirm and establish the reality of the self, and so give comfort to a person torn apart by psychological distress and suffering.

It is also the case, somewhat paradoxically, that the new and unfamiliar can offer comfort. New experiences, new people, and travel have long been seen as ways to comfort a sorrowing person. As the common wisdom holds, new experiences take one out of one's self; when the self is miserable, novelty in the right dosage and context helps to turn attention outward. Work has always been known to be a comfort in the midst of sorrow, because carrying on with one's work and meeting one's obligations offer the consolation of familiar duty and providing new activities that distract.

Since we live complex lives and play many different roles, sometimes those in our more public or professional lives may not know of our private sufferings. Having to go to work and perform while one's heart is breaking can be a form of comfort, because one can become engrossed in meeting the task at hand and thus be temporarily distracted from sorrow. People mourning a parent can function when working among those who do not know of their loss, and someone in the midst of a divorce or family crisis can continue to find comfort in work. Waves of personal sorrow may well up again and again, but there are intervals when the distraction of the performance and role to be played can give some surcease. As someone very wise once said, to save face is to save oneself.

It is also fortunate that even in the midst of our deepest sorrows, when we have been absolutely devastated and are experiencing constant pain and anguish, we can know odd moments of happiness. Strange as it seems, one can laugh or joke in the midst of the deepest suffering—a form of wit aptly known as gallows humor. The humor, goodness, and beauty of life and other people seem able to peneterate every human hell and give flashes here and there of comfort. Human beings are an irrepressible species; this side of psychosis or coma, we display an innate predisposition to take comfort from anything at hand, no matter how horribly we are suffering. Something in us strives to reclaim and recover love and happiness.

Those who have gone through the worst sufferings that one can imagine—the suffering of persecution and betrayal, the agony of prison and concentration camps—have testified to the indestructibility of hope and moments of comfort. Even in the midst of hell, prisoners report taking comfort in the flight of a bird, the work of a spider, the beauty of a sunset—as well as the bravery and indestructibility of the human spirit. No matter how complete the suffering and hellish environment created by oppressors, some comforts and delight in the smallest of things seem impossible to suppress. The larger comforts of loving memories, thoughtful analysis, inner resources of cultural heritage, and religious faith also sustain persons under tortured conditions. If persons can be together in a company, then one will quickly see the resurrection of the comforts of communal life. In the Warsaw ghetto during the worst of the struggles, people still were able to play, celebrate, and engage in religious rites, taking comfort in life together.

The Christian injunction to comfort the sorrowful does not have to work against human nature; there is an innate predisposition to give and receive comfort. Empathy and sympathy are as natural to the human being as selfish survival instincts. Every viable culture reinforces and socializes the young to develop their natural aptitudes to give and take comfort. Thus one finds always and everywhere, customs, rituals, and rites designed to help those who would comfort the sorrowful. The collective institution of custom helps overcome the forces that may inhibit individuals from giving comfort. We know that to comfort another takes energy, attention, time, and effort—that is why it is a form of active love. And inertia, selfishness, and feelings of inadequacy are always present along with altruistic sympathy. Group customs tip the balance in favor of giving comfort by offering patterns to follow and inducing social pressure to overcome inhibitions.

Familiar rituals and formal rites can give great comfort in moments of deep sorrow. Funeral customs have always been an instance of the collective attempt to comfort those who mourn. Today in our pluralistic culture we have many and wide-ranging rites. One dreadful day in our town I went to two equally heartbreaking but very different funeral services. Both families had lost young adult sons, beautiful young men in the prime of their lives, through tragic senseless accidents. One funeral was a traditional Catholic mass with a large Italian family and the whole parish going through the old liturgical rites. The other memorial service was held at a mansion, now used as an educational center, and consisted of friends and family sitting in a living room, giving spontaneous remembrances of the young man and his life. The Catholic mass gave comfort through the familiar formal liturgy that incorporates death into the larger life of the Church and of Creation. The spontaneous informal memorial service gave comfort in the gathering of the company and the opportunity for the ongoing family and circle of friends to express support. Both spontaneity and formal rite were able to provide comfort for those with different temperaments and different belief systems.

Few successful efforts to comfort sorrow attempt to justify or explain the suffering. But at the same time some meaning is given to the sorrow. Why this suffering happened or had to be, is not a question that has to be addressed or fully answered before comforting. Something meaningful can be done about the suffering by offering social support in the present, and inducing hope for the future. Meaning can be discerned and suffering can begin to be transcended even when one recognizes that the suffering is totally unjust and unfair, and no possible explanation can make it right. As Jesus said when healing the man born blind, his blindness was not to be explained or justified by citing any past sin done by him or his parents; rather, the blindness served as an opportunity for the glory of the Lord to be made manifest. We give meaning to suffering by trying to alleviate it through healing love. Even our sufferings can be used for good, if we grow in love and good works.

Christians take comfort from the fact that God can give meaning to suffering by using it for the triumph of love and life. We cannot fully explain evil and suffering, but, by God, we know what to do with it. If we cannot prevent, alleviate, or heal human suffering, we can still triumph over suffering by using it to increase love and life in the world. With God's help we can imitate Jesus, who triumphed through the cross. We also take comfort from the fact that God as a innocent human being also suffered unjust torture and an unfair death as a failure. Jesus was not only tempted as we are, but he suffered as we suffer. We worship a God who understands the human agonies that we experience. The more sensitive the personality, and the more highly developed the self-awareness, the more a person can suffer; it then may well be the case that Jesus suffered more than any other human being ever has. But his suffering also was more triumphantly productive and meaningful than all others. What a comfort and joy it must be for the Lord to know that he has redeemed and liberated the world.

Traditionally, Christians have thought that they can share in the world's liberation by joining their own sufferings to Christ's redemptive suffering. Our greatest comfort and hope would be to see that the senseless human sufferings that cannot be prevented or healed, can still somehow be used by God. Nothing need ever be wasted or lost in Creation's great travail, the childbirth of the Kingdom. Saint Paul voices these ideas in his letters and sees his sufferings as having meaning; his present struggles will be joined with Christ's and so be used by God to work out the world's salvation. Jesus' words in the Gospel about taking up one's cross to follow him imply that our sufferings can be used, as his were, to bring life and love to the world.

Today some Catholic thinkers have tried to reinterpret the idea of redemptive suffering and the belief that the faithful can fill out Christ's suffering. They see a need to correct masochistic devotions of the past, with their exaggerated focus upon the cross, bloody sacrifice, and suffering. They feel the faithful were led to think that God wanted suffering in this life and did not want us to be healthy and happy; the victorious message of the Resurrection and Easter joy was obscured. Perhaps an imbalanced picture did exist in the past, in which the body, the self, the human will were seen solely as enemies of grace to be mortified, scourged, and abnegated. Christian humanism and love of the abundant life Jesus gives us in the present were overcome by a misguided glorification of failure, sacrificial pain, and the world to come.

But revisionists correcting past imbalances can go too far themselves. Christ's obedience unto the cross and his sacrifice is the way we are made one with God, and human suffering is still very much with us. While we realize that God wishes us all to be healthy, happy, and humanly fulfilled, we still have to cope with human suffering in all of its forms. The orthodox emphasis enables us to see meaning in our inevitable sorrows. It makes sense to believe in Christian hope, that God can use our suffering for the good of ourselves, our family, and our friends, and for the transformation of the world.

Our experiences confirm another unfashionable truth. We see that suffering can purify a personality, and can make a person finer, deeper, more understanding, and empathetic— as well as more merry! People full of joy and gratitude often are the same people who have known deep sorrow. There is an old idea that suffering carves out the depths of a personality so that more joy and deeper delights can be contained. At least those who have never suffered often appear superficial, blank, bland, weakened, and out of touch with the human condition. It seems true that "that which does not kill me makes me stronger," as Nietzsche said.

Those who have suffered also appear more driven to struggle against human suffering, having actually known its sting. Admittedly, too much, too early, and too prolonged experiences of suffering can stunt or destroy a person, but when suffering is transcended, it serves to deepen and connect us with our fellow human beings. Sorrow produces a profound need for comfort and it can bring the sufferer closer to God as Mother. Suffering can be turned into a positive impetus for spiritual progress. But to tell a person in sorrow what we have experienced of the long-term uses of suffering is no way to offer comfort. We comfort others in the immediate present by trying to relieve suffering and effect healing, thereby imitating the divine comforter.

Jesus tenderly comforted and healed human beings whenever he could. He desired to comfort more completely the people of Jerusalem, as a mother hen shelters her chicks under her wing. He loved his own, his friends and his people, and he tried to comfort them in the face of death, illness, and other distress. He is shown on the cross comforting those sharing his fate and comforting his mother and beloved disciple. Jesus incarnates the God who in Scripture is shown comforting his people over and over—a bruised reed I will not break nor a flickering wick extinguish. From the beginning to the end God is seen as the great comforter and savior, giving meaning and love's reassurance. God does rescue us from the depths and comforts us in every affliction. In the ultimate Kingdom, God will wipe away every tear, there shall be no more death, no more mourning and sadness. When people say religion is a great comfort to them, they are echoing the testimony of their hearts.

So many times when we go to Mass troubled, sorely beset, and distressed in sorrow, we return home comforted and strengthened. We are comforted by the promise of justice and eternal life in the liturgy, by contemplation of God's goodness and desires for us to be happy, and by the presence of our fellow Christians all struggling on their own journeys, all eating together the bread of life. To comfort also means "to give strength," and worship and prayer do renew us for the daily struggle. Whatever the trouble, whatever the distress, worship, prayer, and fellowship help make it better. We immerse ourselves in an alternate reality where love reigns supreme and we rise up refreshed. A child aroused from the power of a nightmare can be comforted by prolonged reassurances and a walk with a parent around the lighted house—it takes time to reestablish in the consciousness the dominance of the safe daytime world. In the same way, worship reawakens us to God's maternal reality and reassurance.

It is appropriate that adoration of Mary as Mother and the various Marian devotions have long been a comfort for so many Catholics. When God as Mother is obscured by God as avenging Judge, Mary's role reminds us of the maternal love in God's care for us. The wonderful Marian prayers are all prayers that comfort. The repetition, the invocations, the

assurances, the cries to our mother, induce the early dependence and experience of maternal comfort that we remember.
We need such constant reminding because it is always supremely difficult, as John says, to "put our faith in God's love
toward ourselves," and realize the comforting truth that God
is love.

Those strengthened and comforted in the assurance of
God's love are best able to give love and comfort to others in
sorrow. Once again the way we deal with ourselves and God is
entwined with the way we deal with others. One has to be
comfortable to give comfort. When we have been comforted
and have survived our sorrow, we are better able to comfort.
Comfort and joy are the sign of the Spirit's presence and God
as Comforter can give us the heart and power to comfort
others. Love is the motive, love is the message, and love is the
means by which we comfort. The great lovers and saints that
have gone before us have been wonderfully comforting. When
we consider ways to comfort we can look to their example and
to our own experiences.

HOW TO COMFORT

This is perhaps the only case where angels rush in and fools
fear to tread. We should throw ourselves into situations where
the sorrowrful need comfort and try to overcome our hesitan-
cies and our tendency to shrink from the demands of empathy.

We can find many excuses not to offer comfort. Perhaps we
even think of blaming the victim, so that through internal
debate and procrastination the moment passes and we end up
not even trying to offer comfort. Perhaps we should not in-
trude, we tell ourselves, surely there are other people who are
closer than we are. What can we possibly do to help? Won't it
seem intrusive or emotionally false? Of course, if in reality by
some quirk of fate we find that we are not able to help, we can
quickly fade away. Most often our efforts will be welcomed

and appreciated. Each of us can remember, and will remember forever, how good others were when we were comforted in a time of sorrow.

There are times of crises and sorrow when stoic pride, self-reliance, and our horror at being an object of pity no longer matter. Once we have overcome such culturally conditioned feelings and been comforted we can believe that others will welcome our efforts rather than remaining in their isolation. Pride and desires for privacy are better reserved for happy times. After we have been through the mill of life a few times we come to cherish human comfort and realize that strength also lies in being vulnerable, being able gratefully to accept help from others. After receiving comfort we become better at giving it. We learn what works and what doesn't.

The most important thing in giving comfort is to pay attention to the other person. We must enter into the other's inner state and try to grasp his or her experience of sorrow. What feelings, thoughts, and interpretations exist in the other's unique situation? Empathy is a form of reaching out and entering the experience of another person; to really listen and extend one's self takes sustained attention and emotional energy. But when true empathy is achieved, it is wonderfully comforting for the person in pain to know that another person is sharing their inner state. The ability to connect, and to see another through, begins with the ability to reach out and become attuned to the other person.

Mothers seem to attune themselves automatically to their infants. This emotional or affective attunement has been newly studied in developmental psychology and observed to take place in many ways. The mother can show that she is tuned into the inner feelings and emotions of her infant by gesture, rhythmic movements, words, or tone of voice. The message is conveyed that mother understands. When a mother does this as her part in an ongoing dialogue, the infant realizes that another self exists out there and can even share one's inner experience. The infant's sense of inner self is confirmed. The mother's response says, I am here too, I read you, I know how you feel. After this meeting of two selves, a mother may be able to move the dialogue on to other meanings or to different feelings. If the original emotions were sad or fearful, a mother can meet them, confirm her infant's experience, and move on to comfort.

In the same way we must use maternal sensitivity and affective attunement to comfort the sorrowful. One must enter into the person's sad state, attune oneself to their unique experience, slow down, be sorrowful as they are sorrowful. When an insensitive person cannot do this and brusquely insists on dismissing the pain, or puts it aside too quickly with an instant fix, the suffering person is affronted by the lack of understanding. A comforter can only begin to help after he or she has been sufficiently attuned to another's experience. Please, don't do something, just stand there—empathetic presence is what is most needed.

A comforter also has to listen with great attention to understand what is going on in the self's inner dialogue of interpreting and explaining the pain. Perhaps a person is fully in touch with reality and the comforter can simply affirm their interpretation and evaluation of what is happening to them. But perhaps a person is excessively guilty, angry, or despairing, or is projecting in some distorted way. If a comforter can see that a person's explanatory self-dialogue is not in accord with reality, it is part of the comforting role to slowly and gently offer a corrective. Otherwise, sufferers may continue to blame themselves or perpetuate destructive self-imprisonments in illusion. Iron bars do not a prison make, but the mind can thoroughly entrap and cement suffering into a person's inner world.

Of course in offering one's view of reality one also has to be aware of what another person can accept. Again one has to be innocent as a dove and subtle as a serpent. To tell an unbeliever that their suffering can be joined to Christ's redemption of the world, would be stupid as well as intrusively offensive. All effective therapy must be built slowly on what a person can understand at the time and what will reach them where they are. It is always a circular process. One's cognitive interpretations will shape the emotions one feels, and emotional feelings of love and trust will help suffering persons attend to new and less distorted views of reality. Insight therapies, rational-emotive therapies, cognitive therapies, or reframing approaches, relieve suffering by changing the explanations and world view that a person holds. Christians do the same, as do all those persons who have the gift of good counsel.

Perhaps we learn most of our lessons about comforting the sorrowful from our own experiences of tragedy. While one has many experiences over a lifetime there is often a critical incident that makes the most impression. I learned most about comforting those in pain twenty-seven years ago, when the sudden infant death of our fourth son catapulted our young family into crisis and grief. One minute I was a happy nursing mother, with four children, contentedly celebrating my birthday (ironically the feast day of Saint Colette the patron saint of mortally ill infants as well as of Felicity and Perpetua the martyred young mothers). Suddenly, within minutes, I was a grief-stricken young mother streaming tears and milk, in the throes of agony, panic, guilt, and near despair. This searing experience of sudden loss and devastation taught me a great deal.

Some persons we knew were so pained and upset that they could say nothing and so avoided us out of dread of doing or saying the wrong thing. The most successful comforters came and stayed and did not try to explain or justify or interpret, they were simply present to offer love and support. One wonderful woman, the mother of six children herself, heard the news, called a baby-sitter, called a taxi, and came immediately to our house. To grieve together, to share, and to feel the support of friends and neighbors mean everything in a crisis. People also used all the tried-and-true nonverbal ways of giving comfort, bringing food, sending flowers, arranging a funeral mass.

Two thoughtful women friends came and took down the crib and took away all the baby clothes and furniture. Unfortunately, they missed the baby food still in the icebox, nor could anything be done to stem the flow of milk or tears. Wave upon wave of pain overwhelm those who grieve; how much mourning and weeping there is in this valley of tears. Those people who are not upset by a person crying are by far the most comforting: friends who could face death and sorrow as a part of life that can be talked about, were able to talk to me. The priest who came was wonderful in the sense that he was comfortable enough with death to be able to talk about it and give comfort. As fellow Catholics we could affirm some meaning in offering up one's suffering as a sacrifice. Belief in the Resurrection means that death and the desolation of separation cannot be seen as final. Faith does not make the pain less, but it does stave off despair, self-pity, and the temptation to give up on life.

How our family and community rallied to support us! Although everyone who mourns can at times become annoyed at the inadequacy of efforts to relieve pain, still the main response has to be overwhelming gratitude. The horror of being pitied, in need, struck down, and no longer self-sufficient, quickly gave way to thankfulness for the offering of so much love and support. My husband and I clung together along with our three remaining children, all under five. My friends stayed with me for days and suffered through the repetitive compulsion accompanying all traumas, going over and over the circumstances in an effort to finally accept and master what happened. Even my awesome Uncle Tom, a general, wrote an emotional and loving letter. (One is always surprised by the resources people display in a crisis.) He sounded a resurrection theme as old as David's cry in the Old Testament; when David lost his infant son, he voiced his hope that he would go to him and once more see him again after death. Having lost a child makes one sensitive to all similar losses, in the news, among one's friends and family, in Scripture, in literature. Suffering always sensitizes us to similar events. One also takes renewed comfort in the promise that in the future Kingdom of God, there will be no death of infants, and every tear will be wiped away. The belief in immortality and heaven is important for those who lose their loved ones. It is central to our faith to know that our God loves his own and would never leave us alone and lonely.

I also learned how not to comfort by experiencing the unwitting pain that some persons caused when they tried to be consoling. One person did not help when she said that maybe it was better for the baby to die now, since he might have died in an automobile crash as a teenager. The well-meaning lady who said that all infants would be twenty-eight in heaven, seemed in her certitude about the afterlife to be less than reassuring. Nor should we ever tell a sufferer that a disaster is God's will, for who can know? And though it is true that time will heal, no one should be told that at a time of crisis. I have learned never to talk about what might have been or what might be in the future when trying to comfort another's sorrow. Nor should comparisons to other sorrows be offered. An overwhelming situation which brings a person suffering is so present, so uniquely personal, so suffusing of consciousness, that any talk of what might have been, what will be, or what others have suffered can only be seen as a denial and rejection of what is. Even knowing that time does heal and that one will someday recover does not much mitigate present suffering.

It is also important not to cut off one's grieving prematurely. In misguided efforts to be stoic and have faith triumph over misfortune persons can be left with unresolved sadness. I can see now that I should have grieved more and allowed myself to be comforted even more. But as a young person who had mostly experienced triumphs in life, I did not know that one has to thoroughly immerse oneself in a grief and mourn enough to leave a sorrow behind. Nowadays when parents lose children, they are allowed to see and touch and hold the child's body in fully experienced acts of grieving. We have learned a great deal about the pyschology of mourning and grief. Healing takes more time than I allowed. In the past there was an element of trying to deny and undo what happened by prematurely getting up and getting on with life.

Lack of psychological understanding—and a false sense of stoicism, heroism, and the need to be strong—can keep many people from seeking the help that they need to recover thoroughly. Many conscientious souls cannot help but experience a deep sense of guilt for having failed to avert their misfortune. It is far too easy with little-understood and rare occurrences to sink into irrational orgies of self-blame. The residual irrational guilts which many of us carry over from earlier times of our life, can make the comforting of sorrow much more complicated. One has to pay close attention to the inner explanations that a person gives for what has happened. Comforting must always be attuned to external reality as well as the other person's inner state.

A POSTSCRIPT ON OVERCOMFORTING

What if a person brings suffering upon themselves, so that in any moral accounting they deserve the suffering that they experience? What then? Can there be exceptions to our mandate to comfort the sorrowful? Perhaps there are times when the most loving action would be to refrain from attempting to alleviate sorrow; there seem to be cases in which one should not rush to offer comfort. We hear a great deal today about infantilization, overnurturing, enabling, and the necessity of confrontation and tough love. The contention is that you can in reality harm people if you don't let them suffer the consequences of their bad behavior and thereby learn that they can and must help themselves. It seems true that there can be times when someone is suffering good guilt or true remorse, and to try to alleviate their immediate pain would be counterproductive for them in the long run. They may need the pain to be in touch with reality, and to be induced to change and amend their life. The prodigal son suffered in many instructive ways before he came to his senses and decided to return home and restore his life to happiness.

The need to suffer valid consequences is emphasized in much of the self-help and how-to-help-others literature. The philosophy of Alcoholics Anonymous and the books for women who love too much are examples of this message. Many other books on dealing with people with drug problems or coping with rebellious adolescents have talked of reality therapy and learning to give tough love. Tough love is based on letting people grow up and take responsibility for the real consequences of their own behavior. Many people have always had persons who have protected and enabled them to keep on hurting and harming themselves and others. The overnurturing parent, spouse, or employer constantly assumes responsibility and shelters the guilty or sick person from the consequences of his or her behavior.

The suffering and sorrow necessary to learn responsibility or to be impelled to seek help, may never be fully experienced or confronted. A delinquent child, drug addict, or abusing spouse is never forced to learn what other people have learned. Ironically, a nurturing caretaker's natural urge to rescue can become an impediment to wise nurture. A rescue fantasy, or a desire to excise another's pain once it has become too much for us to bear, can sometimes impel us to do overprotective things that enable the other person to continue on a self-destructive course. In these situations a person who truly loves another has to be strong enough to allow another's pain and sorrow to be experienced. Comfort would be only false comfort.

One other exception to the mandate to comfort arises when someone uses unhappiness and sorrow to hide from other emotions. Sometimes depression, sorrow, and a sense of failure serve a hidden purpose in an individual's life. There is a need to be unhappy, a need for failure, and a clinging to sorrow so that one will not have to face other aspects of one's life, such as justifiable anger, fear of success, or a drive to achieve more. Any number of things can be hidden: the fear of being envied, the fear of living more fully and joyously, and so on. Psychologists have found that sorrow is used often as a self-defeating strategy and is quite different from the way it may appear on the surface. In such cases to comfort the sorrower and not see the other underlying factors would be to support the stunting of a person instead of challenging them to grow in a new way.

Fairly subtle problems of discernment can arise. Confronted with a person's suffering, we must ask whether this is a case where the sorrow should be challenged or unmasked? Is this a sorrow that needs to be felt and experienced in order for the person to grow up and mature? Or is this a sorrow that comes to all people, could never be avoided, and should simply be comforted as an act of love for another? As always in trying to love wisely, one has to discern by careful attention and listening exactly to what is happening in a person's inner life. Sometimes the very best thing one can do for others is to challenge them or help them let their sorrow go. Sometimes the best thing that one can do for others is to let them truly sorrow and grieve. They may need to allow themselves to fully experience the pain for the first time in an extended way.

Such problems of discernment will never be solved easily.

One guide may be how much someone can do on their own about reversing the situation or the events that are creating their sorrow. Some things can simply never be undone. Those people who have done horrible deeds and are sorrowing, or those people who have brought upon themselves dreadful fates, should be fully sympathized with and comforted when they repent. In the end one looks to the example of God and Jesus, who seem to reach out to everyone good, bad, or indifferent and offer love and comfort. Perhaps we should always err when in doubt on the side of offering as much comfort and love as we can. In our individualistic selfish culture we should probably take our chances with offering comfort until we have clear evidence that it is harming another. After all the God whose love we seek to imitate never fails and constantly goes beyond reasonable bounds in loving us.

In the end the greatest comfort is knowing that no matter what, God loves us. As Saint Paul says the one thing certain is that nothing can separate us from the love of Christ. A true comforter will offer love in a thousand different ways, over and over, with subtlety and finesse. Love provides the ultimate meaning of life and if we cannot understand why or how things are working out, we can understand what it is to be loved. Some of the greatest mystics have repeated over and over very simple words of comfort. Dame Julian of Norwich constantly reminds us, "All will be well, all will be well." She invokes Christ as mother and reassures us of God's maternal care. If we are truly loved everything can be borne.

5

TO BEAR WRONGS
PATIENTLY

*If you put up with suffering for doing what is right, this is
acceptable in God's eyes. It was for this you were called, since
Christ suffered for you in just this way and left you an example, to have you follow in his footsteps. He did no wrong; no
deceit was found in his mouth. When he was insulted he
returned no insult. When he was made to suffer, he did not
counter with threats. Instead, he delivered himself up to the
One who judges justly. (1 Peter 2:20–25)*

To bear wrongs patiently. In an age of liberation movements,
revolution, and assertiveness training this work of mercy
makes us wince at its apparent endorsement of fatalism and
masochism. Have not generations of the poor and oppressed
been kept down and made submissive by the idea that they
should bear wrongs patiently? Today, we do not see patience
as a virtue; it is impossible to imagine parents naming their
daughter Patience in admiration of the attitude. Patience now
is equated more often with passivity and long-suffering, an
undesirable condition to be overcome.

Part of our problem with patience may stem from our
American spirit. America has always been the land of ideal
supermen who run faster than a speeding bullet. We are the
people who wish to hurry up everything and provide instant
relief, in medication, in fast food, in the fast-track career. At
the same time we are programmed *not* to stand for wrongs, or
as one state motto warns, "Don't Tread on Me." If you do, you
will be instantly sorry. We won't tolerate delay, obstacles, or
oppression—"Give me liberty or give me death," right this

second. We believe that the impossible can only take a little longer; individual liberty and rights to self-defense (enabled by the possession of guns) are our paramount values. This American cultural conditioning makes it difficult for us to relate to spiritual counsels commending patience.

Feminists, blacks, American Indians, and other oppressed groups have also balked at traditional spiritual interpretations of the need for patience. Accepting suffering and injustice in the name of love has been labeled the "Uncle Tom response" that holds back liberation movements. Induced female masochism has been seen as a chief obstacle to women's progress. Indeed, masochism is much on our mind these days and has long since escaped its narrower meaning connected with sexuality. Masochism in its general cultural form applies to persons who are apathetic, resigned to suffering, and expect poor treatment from others. Their self-defeating behavior correlates with a low sense of self-worth, an inadequate sense of personal rights, and a lack of hope that things can change for the better. Who am I to deserve more or make waves? I am doomed to suffer, and besides, as a suffering victim, I may be able to garner some psychological advantages for myself, or at least avoid danger.

Self-defeating behavior can become a way of life. The martyred, long-suffering mother, the put-upon wife, the overburdened worker or middle manager—even male versions are available. Psychoanalysts have described lives in which a person manifests a persistent need for failure or the idealization of unhappiness. One can observe regularly the puzzling cases of the competent persons who, despite their innate capacity, can never quite make it and who repeatedly self-destruct, snatching defeat after defeat from the jaws of victory. An unconscious or preconscious program or script appears to have been established in early life such that unhappiness and defeat appear psychologically necessary for safety and security. Success, happiness, or victory may have become identified as dangerous for unconscious reasons—fears of provoking retaliatory jealousies or losing love, and guilt over outshining one's parental figures. Only personal defeat, suffering, and inhibition feel safe.

In self-deprecating long-suffering, a person defensively adopts the habit of abnegation. Is this psychological condition the same as bearing wrongs patiently? No; neither masochism nor fatal resignation are meant when Christians speak of bearing wrongs patiently. Christians believe that fatalism can be fatal, indeed a form of despair. When one gives up hope, self-respect, and a sense of internal agency, one gives up the struggle to change. We cannot make the Kingdom come when we have become resigned to suffering and think that nothing we can do will make any difference. We need to reconsider patience, and rethink what it means to bear wrongs patiently. How is this activity related to love? What is patience? What are wrongs?

WRONGS

What are wrongs? How does a wrong differ from injuries or from sins, the other negative things that we must cope with in the traditional list of the spiritual works of mercy. As compared to injury or sin, a wrong seems more general, less specific, less intentional, less often directed with premeditated malice toward a particular individual. The time framework is also different, in that wrongs often are long-term chronic conditions as compared to acute attacks or brief episodes. A wrong is more socially institutionalized and impersonal. Wrongs are definitely immoral and unethical in the sense that the innocent suffer, but they lack the characteristic of specific injury or specific intentional rejections of God through consciously evil action. Things should be otherwise, should be just—some things are unfair, unjust, terrible—but wrongs seem less personal than either sin or injuries.

Examples of wrongs to bear might include prejudice against one's race, sex, religion, age, class, or condition. To be subject to dislike as a member of a stigmatized group would be an example of a wrong or violation of justice. This wrong would not be directed at oneself specifically but would be a form of structural social oppression. We can think of many wrongs that exist even in our relatively free American society. To be old and denigrated is certainly one wrong that many in the society can look forward to. To be poor, homeless, or deprived of health care or other basic needs and rights is also a wrong. Other wrongs one might have to cope with include being imprisoned wrongfully, being dismissed from a job unjustly, and being wronged in some other transaction with the world or social system. Wrongs and injustice also arise from human errors, flaws, and failings.

Wrongs do not include acts of nature such as earthquakes, floods, or disease. One could not say that one has been wronged by an earthquake or pneumonia. Of course if one has intentionally been given a disease, such as AIDS, by someone who through deception spread the infection, then one could consider the suffering incurred as a wrong. Wrongs are essentially social betrayals and failings toward an individual, infringments upon justice, equality, and human dignity. In countries where one can be arrested, imprisoned, or tortured without recourse to the law there are, of course, many more wrongs to be borne. We are indeed fortunate to live in a society that does not require most of us to bear as much injustice as most people have had to bear.

But, say the skeptics, America is a land in which justice more or less prevails because Americans have never accepted the counsel that we should accept wrongs patiently. Have we not always taken arms against a sea of troubles, with the firm conviction that we could overcome difficulty and injustice through effort. The idea that God helps those who help them-selves and that human beings can solve their own problems, has been at the root of our satisfactory condition of life. We have always been willing to fight for our rights. Not for us the sentimental glorification of suffering, or the excusing of failure and retreat! We are the can-do people who will try ever harder when an obstacle or wrong is in our way.

BEARING WRONGS

But does *bearing a wrong* mean passively accepting the wrong? Not when we pay attention to the meaning of *to bear*. To bear means "to support and move, to carry, to sustain, to hold up, conduct oneself in a given manner," and, of course, it also means "to produce a child." These are all intensely active human functions. Bearing is not passive after all; weak deli-cate persons given to apathy or masochism cannot bear up, cannot bear down, cannot bear much of anything. Other active meanings of bear are "to exercise as a power" and "to assume something." All of these activities take strength and depths of human resources. The power to sustain something, assume something, or bring something forth, requires strength and courage. This has nothing to do with fatalism or passive submission.

Once we see that bearing is an active exercise of power, we can begin to understand what we are called to do in this spiritual work of mercy. To bear wrongs patiently is an active enabling form of love and power. It is having the firmness to hold ourselves and others up, through strain, stress, and evil times, without causing more suffering and evil. One can best see this spiritual work of mercy as a call for toughness, strength of will, and strength of purpose. It is a display of firmness and fortitude rather than weakness. Is one strong enough to bear trials, to bear up when things are not working out, when things are not going one's way, when one is being oppressed or having to suffer unmerited wrongs? Passive, weak persons faced with difficulties either collapse or are driven to violent outbursts in which the wrong done them is taken out on others. Self-pity and tantrums, including the tantrums of sullen silence, are often the reaction of the childishly immature. They pass on their distress to others, often with violent abuse, and thereby multiply injustice, escalate misfortune, and magnify the amount of suffering and evil in the world.

How well one bears the wrongs one encounters in life is a true test of strength of character. Some wrong will have to be faced by almost everyone, since injustice is inherent in the disorder of the present world. If we cannot bear wrongs with fortitude, we fail in our responsiblity toward those with whom we live. Everyone knows those who cannot bear stress, who cannot cope when obstacles or problems arise. Often they are people who have never had to struggle before, or people who, despite superficial indulgences, seem not to have gotten enough love or discipline.

A person needs past experience in coping in order to be able to cope when injustice or wrongs are encountered later. This aptitude seems to have less to do with physical health or strength than with psychological attitude. A certain humility, gratitude, and sense of reality is needed. When one is still a childish, self-engrossed, narcissistic person, one demands that the world conform to one's whims and wishes. Everything one encounters should be fair, just, comfortable, and instantly solvable. When reality does not oblige, the immature person disintegrates. Or alternatively, a person who has struggled to succeed, can become gradually corrupted by power, comfort, and flattery so that he or she falls into narcissistic expectation of omnipotence. A person with power can begin to ignore reality and the needs of others, slowly regressing to infancy over the course of four or five decades. Psychological strength is revealed by how well a person is able to cope over the long haul.

It is instructive to look at extreme cases in which people have had to bear wrongs, cases all too prevalent in our modern era of concentration camps, preventive detention, disappearances, and torture. Victor Frankl, the noted psychologist who was incarcerated in the Nazi concentration camps during the Second World War, was one of the first to draw pertinent pyschological and spiritual conclusions from his observation of individuals in extreme situations. He saw that persons react to stress and persecution partly in common patterns determined by the horrible situation; but, more crucially, their behavior was also partly determined by their individual character. Some people were not able to cope, or bear up under the pressure. They broke down morally, spiritually, and physically. Others mustered the strength to keep their humanity alive in the grim situation, while still others were truly heroic. As Frankl reflects, "It becomes clear that the sort of person the prisoner became was the result of an inner decision, and not the result of camp influences alone." There were always decisions to be made:

> "Every hour offered the opportunity to make a decision, a decision which determined whether you would or would not submit to those powers which threatened to rob you of your very self, your inner freedom: which determined whether or not you would become the plaything of circumstance, renouncing freedom and dignity to become molded into the form of a typical inmate."*

Personal attitude makes the difference in situations of stress. Wrongs that we encounter will offer this test, this challenge of whether we will be conformed to the world or will be able to overcome through our inner resistance. We

Man's Search for Meaning (New York: Simon & Schuster, 1963), p. 104.

bear up and sustain and carry wrongs because we believe with Frankl that "man can preserve a vestige of spiritual freedom, of independence of mind even in such terrible conditions of psychic and physical stress." The poeple who have experienced the worst demonstrate that "everything can be taken from a man but one thing: the last of the human freedoms—to choose one's attitude in any given set of circumstances, to choose one's own way." When people give up choosing, give up hope, they can no longer cope psychologically, nor long survive physically.

Despair is born in many ways. One of the most insidious ways is through acquiescence in one's mind to the claims and world view of those who inflict the wrongs. To be persuaded by and accept the viewpoint of one's oppressors or torturers, to give up one's inner moral and spiritual resistance to evil, breaks the human spirit. As one young woman poet writes of her struggle to resist the guards in her Siberian prison, "Well, we'll live as the soul directs, not asking for other bread." If one begins to inwardly accede to evil, if one becomes callous to the wrongs inflicted upon oneself and others, then the oppressor has won a convert to their system of injustice and immorality. In the Gulag prisons, as the young poet proclaims, it is "the best in all the world, the most tender, who don't break." Their virtue, tenderness, and alertness to the unjust wrongs being inflicted upon the innocent, help them withstand torture and bear wrongs without succumbing. Those who harden break because they no longer care enough to nurture and support themselves or other sufferers.

It is important to remember that Christians, knowing that they are made in God's image and redeemed at great cost, are instructed to admonish sinners and to struggle as in childbirth so that God's love and justice can be born in the creation. However it is obvious that success can never be achieved instantly. Before the final victory one must be able to bear the wrongs that still exist in the midst of the struggle. This is true in the political communities and the larger social groups in which we live, and it is also true as we struggle and work out our salvation together in family and personal life. It is essential to get the right balance.

One must bear wrongs patiently while at the same time admonishing, resisting, and working to right the wrongs. Bearing wrongs patiently is not an instance of religion serving as the opiate of the people, or pie in the sky when you die. It has nothing to do with a pietism that retreats from the world in order to avoid conflict. In fact the spiritual resistance to injustice may precipitate or increase conflict: struggles to overcome evil with good are not compatible with certain gnostic approaches to life in which evil is thought not to exist and wrongs suffered are only an illusion. In the tradition of the Old Testament prophets, we must accept the presence of evil and recognize injustice before we can bear it or initiate change.

A belief that the status quo represents a just world has been seen by psychologists as the royal road to blaming victims and abdicating social responsibility. Since there is something in us that wants the world to be just, the temptation is always there to believe that the world is just. If the world were just, the victors would deserve their spoils and the losers would deserve what they get. When persons believe this it meets all sorts of psychological needs. If victims have somehow brought suffering on themselves, our responsibility to help them is lessened. The rest of us in a just world can also more easily deny that we, too, could be victimized. This belief serves as a protection against accepting the irrationality and injustice that exist in life. How upsetting it is to realize the truth that good people have terrible things happen to them that they certainly never deserved.

To face the disorder of the world produces deep anxiety. We try to deny it. But the counsel to bear wrongs patiently helps break through our denials by reiterating and reminding us that wrongs do exist and that the innocent and righteous suffer. We belong to the human community who endure unmerited wrongs. We cannot avoid it, nor separate ourselves from the unlucky persons who suffer.

PATIENCE

Patience is an active exercise of power. Patience is to be expectant, to act strongly without complaint, to act with equanimity. It is the ability to continue efforts undisturbed by obstacles, delays, or the temptation to quit. Perseverance and patience are related. To expect that victory and success will come in the long run is the basis of patience and perseverance. And perseverance, as Saint Paul points out, brings hope. The activity of *keeping on* keeping on produces the change in viewpoint. One's own activity reveals to oneself and others that activity is possible. Each step that one takes changes one's position in the world.

One is patient because one believes in the future and in the ultimate victory of good. As Christ was sure of God, the One who judges justly, he could return good for evil. The ultimate triumph of justice means that one can be patient as one makes interim efforts. As Saint Teresa of Avila said, "Patience obtains all . . . all things pass, God alone suffices." When we look at the patience of the saints imitating the patience displayed by Jesus, who bore his wrongs with calmness, equanimity, and courage, we see that they were all able to act in this way because of their utter confidence in the ultimate outcome and victory. God's will *will* be done, justice *will* come. In the end all wrongs will be righted by God's power. This belief that the Kingdom will triumph and that in the end a new Jerusalem will be created gives the assurance and power to bear wrongs in the present with patience.

Victor Frankl also observed that only those people who were able to discern meaning in their suffering and thus sustain hope were able to bear wrongs patiently. To see meaning in their suffering meant that they could bear it without despair. Christians are not the only ones who have had the ability to be patient and bear wrongs; other believers have also been certain of meaning in life. Marxists and communists, for instance, have seen themselves contributing to the inevitable forces of history—and they, too, held up well in concentration camps. All believers in transcendent meaning are given strength in the present by their belief in ultimate spiritual vindication. The American Indians who could sing their victory songs while being tortured were as great a witness to the psychology of conviction as were the Jesuit martyrs whom the Indians tortured. Both groups believed that their courage was not wasted.

The conviction that suffering is not wasted helps us to act bravely and bear wrongs patiently. The ultimate despair in the modern world arises from the fact that nothing seems to have meaning when "the best have lost all conviction." Then the wrongs that we suffer are simply random occurrences in a chaotic world that has no purpose and no connection with ultimate values. This lack of meaning leads to the collapse of young persons and adolescents who so often commit suicide in the midst of material abundance. They have no sense of meaning, no sense that the wrongs they must bear might have a connection to the rest of the universe. Without a hope that God can use their suffering in some way or that they can transcend this suffering or that ultimately the forces of right will triumph, they despair and end their lives. It's also important to note that few children today are ever instructed in the virtue of patience. In a world in which immediate satisfaction is touted (go for it, and so on), where would one find a model of patience that would be admirable to a young person?

With patience we can work to right wrongs, but we know that it cannot happen immediately. Even Christians confident of final victory still have to get through the intermediate time between now and then. While we are patient in hope and trust that eventually justice will triumph, what should be our attitude toward those who are working with us, or toward those who are the oppressors, and who are creating the wrongs which we have to bear? If we take seriously both the commandment to love and the need to forgive the sins of those who oppress us, there is only one answer to this question. We must be patient and full of graciousness, kindliness, and positive joyful strength. The other alternatives are sullen apathy or varying degrees of rage.

When one gives into wrath, anger, and—even worse—bitter resentment, it means that the enemy or the oppressor has conquered one inside as well as outside. When one hates an oppressor, the outer coercion that one cannot prevent has overcome one's inner freedom as well. Patience differs from masochism: masochists who suffer entrap themselves in the suffering insofar as they feel that they should be suffering, should be unhappy, and are unworthy to be happy. But those who bear a wrong patiently know that it is unjust, know that it is wrong for this wrong to be existing, and yet refuse to let this wrong make them miserable or enraged. When one is patient one can be joyful in the midst of the oppression. A heart that is filled with love and kindness toward one's self, toward one's fellow victims, and toward one's oppressors cannot be counted as crushed. This magnanimity and kindliness and graciousness produce the spirit of a person who is a victor and no longer a victim. It is the ultimate triumph of the inner spirit over the wrongs being inflicted. But, of course, such a victory is not easy to achieve.

Here, again, an extreme case history can be instructive to us in meeting the challenges of more ordinary experience. A woman who had been tortured in a Russian prison reported on her struggle to find an effective way to respond. As she was being subjected to systematic torture by an expert at breaking down every defense she searched for ways to find meaning in her absurd and horrible situation. When she tried to shrink into a negative posture the torturer came on stronger as bullies usually do when they sense weakness. However, if she tried to fight back in anger she also whetted his sadistic appetite. In the midst of this she prayed and tried to permeate the situation with spiritual consciousness. With this she felt that she began to understand the other person's self in a new way. But if she became in the least sentimental or overly indulgent toward her torturer, he would brutalize her all the more. Also if she became self-pitying or overindulgent of herself, again displaying weakness, the same thing happened. Slowly she found a balance between indulgence on either side, a way of serenity that she felt was founded on the "divine rock." In the presence of God within her, the core of her personality and foundation, she was able to find the strength to resist and transcend each new act of brutality. She was so grounded in God that she grew perfectly quiet despite the pain. Realizing that he could not disrupt her serenity the torturer lost interest—the sadist was freed from his obsession and she was freed by her centeredness in God.

Now most persons will never be tortured in prison, but many people have had to bear unavoidable psychological persecution in some form, often from a family member. A person under the influence of alcohol, a person being cruel in defense of his or her anxiety or guilt, or a person trying to avoid emptiness and depression can actively persecute a friend or family member.

Just as in physical torture, there can be malice and efforts to confuse and to cause pain through lies and verbal abuse. The effort can also be made to destroy a person's sense of self and confidence in their perception of reality. Objective reality threatens the psychological torturer's power, so it must be distorted by every means at hand. When this horrible kind of suffering and wrong is visited upon an individual the only defense is to seek the serenity and spiritual centeredness that can give one the power to patiently bear the wrongful persecution. In ordinary circumstances one has to seek the same balance as a person under physical torture: one can neither be indulgent and superficially forgiving of what the other person is doing nor self-pitying and self-defeating, wallowing in sweet sorrow. It is necessary to seek confidence in oneself as God's child, and confidence in one's view of the world and reality. Centeredness on God gives the patience and love needed for detachment and the transcendence of anger and bitterness.

Many of the self-help books and self-help movements that have helped so many sufferers teach the same spiritual lessons of unsentimental love and balanced detachment. A well-known example of this is the famous serenity prayer of Alcoholics Anonymous which beseeches God to grant me the serenity to accept that which I cannot change, the courage to change that which I can, and the wisdom to know the difference. This serenity is a form of patience for those who cannot avoid suffering a wrong; it helps them to center themselves and not be consumed by bitterness and the fruitless effort to change and control the uncontrollable.

Other self-help books take a similar spiritual approach. They emphasize praying for the persons who are provoking so much sorrow and trouble, thereby letting them go in order to center upon oneself and one's own spiritual affirmations and belief. This "letting go" through the cultivation of patience includes love, detachment, hope, and confidence in one's own view of reality. Bearing wrongs patiently gives peace and an ability to survive and bear the unbearable one day at a time. If one fights back and becomes angry and wrathfully obsessed with the other's wrongdoing, one allows the persecutor and oppressor to be victorious. Once again, they have made you play their game, and you lose. By fighting back one also sustains the distracting game in which wrongdoers can take refuge and justify themselves. Instead of facing their own difficulty, their own wrong, and the reality of their own behavior, they have in their victim's counterattacks and reactive anger a continuing excuse for their own aggression. All oppressors and wrongdoers love to provoke violence so that their own suppressions and original violence will seem justified to themselves and to others.

If one keeps one's serenity and lives up to Christ's example of patience and love, then no matter what happens one's inner spirit has not been violated by aggresive hate. It is what actively comes out of a person that defiles and disintegrates personality, not what is done to a person without consent.

It is also the case that bearing wrongs patiently may be the most prudent and shrewd course of action to accomplish one's goal. When Christ says that the meek will inherit the earth, he may be making a descriptive statement as well as giving spiritual counsel. A Christian does not bear wrongs patiently *in order* to be more successful in the world, but it often turns out to be an effective life strategy. Even those who do not share the Christian motivation have championed the advantages of nonviolent strategies to achieve certain goals. If they are not innocent as doves, they are at least wily as the serpent.

WHY THE MEEK MAY INHERIT THE EARTH

Bearing wrongs patiently may work better than anything else one can do in a struggle or conflict. It works because in order to plan and think effectively, one must be calm and able to take time to assess all the factors in any situation. Wrath and anger and the gusts of near madness one might feel when being mistreated can keep one from being able to think clearly or see the oppressor or aggressor as they really exist, that is, from their own stance and point of view as well as from one's own viewpoint. Bearing wrongs patiently has sometimes been interpreted as meaning to bear with wrongdoers patiently, and this larger understanding is important.

While trying to support and love an oppressor one will cultivate empathy and take account of his role as he sees it. This alternate point of view keeps one from subjectively overestimating or underestimating the other's power or position, as hate and fear induce one to do. What is important to this other person or to this other group's world view? What in his system is being threatened in our particular conflict or struggle? Loving my enemy I must pay sustained attention to his point of view; through careful attention I will inevitably and easily penetrate psychologically to his goals, fears, strengths, and weaknesses. As the mother knows her child, and the lover knows the beloved, so I can know my oppressor through sustained empathetic efforts to love him.

Once I know through patience what I could never know through violent hate, I can better devise a means to solve our problems. Love is creative in its free play of the mind, while hate narrows thinking into the obsessive circuits around revenge. If I would seek the best for my enemy along with the best for me and mine, I must be free, confident, and loving in my strategic actions. I can enter a dialogue willingly, for I, too, am concerned with what will serve my oppressor's best interests, including, of course, his moral well-being as well as pyschological and material welfare. If he is ensnared in wrongdoing and injustice, I want to help liberate him. How can we together use what Gandhi called soul-force and truth-force to lead us to a new creative solution that will do justice to us both? When my opponent sees that I am concerned about him as well as steely in my concern for justice for myself and my people, new options become possible.

Gandhi said that means are ends in the making, and this is certainly true when one is bearing wrongs and struggling to right them. If you foment acts of aggressive violence, or collapse in self-pity back into fatalism and masochism, there is little hope for a new peaceful future. Violence begets more violence, masochism invites sadism, apathy begets inertia. If I do what my enemy does in retaliation, I become my enemy. Violent revolutionaries who come to power repress in their turn.

We are just beginning to plumb the resources of nonviolent social action in the world today. The civil-rights movement, Solidarity in Poland, the Philippine revolution, and other grassroots campaigns for peace and justice are pointing to new realities of the way power is exercised. Power always depends to some extent on the cooperation of others. Waging peace instead of war is slowly becoming a real option in the world. But training and mobilizing for nonviolent action may take more discipline and sustained effort than old-fashioned warfare. What remains to be seen is whether such strategies can work without prolonged efforts to achieve high levels of collective spiritual discipline. What works for individuals and small communities should be adaptable to larger numbers but it will be a challenge to devise strategies for a whole society.

LEARNING TO BEAR WRONGS PATIENTLY—CULTIVATING PATIENCE

For a Christian, progress in bearing wrongs patiently can only mean growing in wisdom and truth. Becoming more Christlike in our own lives is the only Way to go. Once one has tried to do good to enemies and had the bitter experience of failure, one is forced to admit that it is impossible without God's help. God wins, because we learn that one cannot learn to bear wrongs patiently without being sustained and transformed by God. Only through the empowerment of Christ and the Holy Spirit helping us from within the depths of our personality can we cultivate the centeredness to become patient. We need a great deal of meditation and quiet prayer. At the same time we must have worship in community, participating in the sacraments to strengthen the bonds and beliefs which give us faith that justice will come. Only love begets love. If we do not patiently grow in love among our own that we see daily, we surely will not be able to love wrongdoers who oppress us.

We must also cultivate loving patience toward ourselves. We have to be patient with ourselves before we can be serene and patient with others. As with all our spiritual transactions, the way we treat others is intimately tied to the way we treat ourselves, which depends in turn on our relationship to God, the ground of reality. Bearing our own faults, and limiting our own self-destructiveness and suffering are prerequisites for bearing the faults of others and supporting them so their wrongdoing is limited. We can overcome evil only by good, through the real and deep understanding that God loves us and accepts us just as we are. With all our faults and failings we are not able to bring about instant justice and right all wrongs immediately. It takes time for the leaven of patience to work, for the seed to grow. Once we understand that God lovingly accepts our efforts and will bring about final victory, we can accept ourselves more completely. We know we're not perfect and that we fail often, just like those whose wrong-doing we must patiently bear. Perhaps one of the best ways to think about ourselves and our oppressors as we bear wrongs patiently is that we are all developing and growing—hard as that is.

All creation is groaning to be born and trying to come to the fruition that God desires. We now know that the universe is hurtling through space and that expansive change is the only constant surrounding us. However, certain things, such as our bodies and many of the material things around us are changing at such a slow rate that they seem hardly to change at all. So, too, the wrongs that we are trying to right can seem unchangeable, but if we think about the history of our world and the fact that so much change has already taken place over the centuries we gain hope and patience. Seemingly permanent structures are really only temporary crystallizations, slower in their transformations than other aspects of the universe. Our bones seem solid compared to the food that we eat but this is only because our bones change more slowly. So, too, with the mountains and the inner core of the molten earth, as well as with the explosions of the stars—everything we know from science points to a universe of perpetual movement. I make all things new, says the Lord. Surely the human spirit and our social consciousness and social worlds are also in motion.

But nothing in our human sphere happens without human effort. Only after working can we rest in God, and after rest and restoration we return to work out our salvation. We must prepare the ground of our personality so that God can act through us. This preparation and pruning require discipline. Discipline and the tools of discipline that many have spoken of are ways of training and painfully pruning, so that we are able to live in fuller happiness and joy in the long run. We cannot become patient without a certain amount of discipline and asceticism; it is the training that is necessary to run in the race. We have to learn delayed gratification. We have to learn to give up illusions and fantasy for the sake of truth and reality, and we have to learn to admit our responsibility for those things that we do and cause. We also have to become flexible and no longer rigidly fixed on perfection and the desire for absolute control. We would like to be gods—we constantly thirst after perfect and absolute order according to our will. Training ourselves in patience and serenity is much like training the body for sports. It is slow. It requires constant individual effort combined with constant reliance upon creative forces beyond us to bring about a new birth.

It is instructive to remember that in actual childbirth a form of patience is also the best of all strategies. Similar principles seem to operate in pain management. To fight the pain or to fight the body's birth contractions, to flail about in fear and

loathing, to writhe and grimace and struggle, makes the pain
more horrible and intense. The way to conquer is through
acceptance of the body and through efforts to transform what
is happening. One must concentrate mentally and simul-
taneously exert controlled efforts to relax in order to float
through the process as a swimmer rides a wave. The body
seems to follow certain laws that operate in the psyche as well.
According to the "law of least effort," it is better not to
struggle and focus upon a goal, but to focus upon something
else and imperceptibly float toward one's goal bit by bit. In
trying *not* to do things one should not focus upon the thing
one does not want to do, since that only brings it to mind
more acutely and makes it more difficult to resist.

The best way to bear pain and to bear wrongs is to jog along
patiently, in a sense of moment-to-moment calmness and
acceptance, attending to the good, and confident of eventual
victory. Struggling to control a chaotic situation can only
result in pain, frustration, and stress. Some unfortunate personalities (those with so-called type-A behavior) spend their
lives struggling against the constraints of time, the frustrations
and obstacles of matter, and the inability of the world to
function perfectly. Their driven quality produces intense
stress, making these persons irritable and more subject to
heart disease and other stress-related diseases.

So many persons in our society suffer physically and psychologically because they have never learned even the first
lessons of patience. It is such an un-American virtue. We are
all too familiar with the experience of burnout, in which
people struggling to help others and to right wrongs simply
have to give up and quit. They have not been able to persevere
in patience and hope because of the continuing frustration of
their desire to see wrongs righted; they become angry, irritable, and emotionally drained; finally a condition of emotional
numbing is induced. Such numbing can happen to idealistic
teachers, nurses, social workers, health workers, and others

who must struggle against injustice and the wrongs of the world.

When techniques for "stress reduction" are offered to over-stressed modern persons, they turn out to be secularized versions of spiritual techniques and spiritual disciplines. One changes behavior by changing thoughts and feelings, and one changes thoughts and feelings by changing behavior—all at the same time. Imagery, behavioral rehearsals, and physical strategies involving breathing exercises and health habits are used to help persons relax and to restore their sense of well-being. How hard it is for Americans to cultivate serenity, when it is so alien to our culture and to our most admired heroes!

It takes a long time to discipline the mind and the heart and the body. While techniques such as role playing or behavioral rehearsal sound like mere jargon, they are simply old and tested means of using the human imagination to help become the way one wishes to be. By playing out new scripts and scenarios, either actually or in one's mind, one can prepare for future challenges. Watching films of the best tennis moves improves one's next game. Liturgical re-creations of the Gospel inspire one's next moves in a larger game. The spirituality of Saint Ignatius, in concert with many other schools of spirituality, have known all about the power of imagination.

But alas, one cannot simply perform one's way to inner spiritual strength. We really cannot do this alone. For the Christian, the path to such strength must include prayer and worship and actual practice of certain kinds of virtues. Only through practice and the deeds that produce new habits of the heart can God act to transform us into the selves we wish to be. Christians change themselves by asking God to transform them: Give us a new heart, one that is no longer apathetic and hardened. Indeed, make us desire to be given a new heart capable of love. When we have grown in God's love, we will be able to bear wrongs patiently.

6

TO FORGIVE ALL INJURIES

Bear with one another: forgive each other as soon as a quarrel begins. The Lord has forgiven you; now you must do the same. (Colossians 3:13–14)

To forgive all injuries—this spiritual work of mercy may be the most difficult of them all. If every spiritual work of mercy is an act of love freely undertaken by a person's conscious self, this particular work is the hardest to come by naturally. Human beings do not forgive easily. Indeed, most legal and moral systems do not ask people to forgive injuries—as though recognizing it to be an impossible task. Among certain pagan religions it was even an impiety to forgive an enemy, especially an enemy who has harmed one's kin or country. Forgiving an enemy would have been seen as craven cowardice and an affront to the gods, who rightly demand vengeance and blood sacrifice.

The more common moral norm in the human species seems to be the crude justice of an "eye for an eye," "a tooth for a tooth." This attempt to establish an equilibrium of hurt and retaliatory payment seems to satisfy some deep and primitive concept of fairness. Those who make others suffer should suffer equally in return; appropriate retribution should be meted out as a debt should be repaid. Small children immediately take to this approach, with little or no instruction. "It's only fair," says the child; harm that has been done should be repaid by equal punishment for the offender. This strong innate feeling for the rightness of retributive justice still fuels our legal system and the recurring campaigns to retain or restore capital punishment. A life for a life—nothing else will do. A person should suffer in equal measure for horrible crimes committed against the innocent.

Satisfying the natural thirst for just retribution for wrong-doing, can serve socially to control the equally natural human lust for revenge. Persons can long for a totally destructive vengeance in which tenfold harm is returned for an injury. If you kill one of ours, we will wipe out your whole family, your people, and your country, plowing over your fields with salt. The desire to take excessive vengeance is also natural to the human heart. At least fair retribution combined with the safeguards of due process restrict human aggression and desire for immediate vengeance. The lynch mob or feuding clan must bow to the authority of the courts and the law; this is as much justice as most societies can manage.

Fairness may even be programmed into the natural order. It has been shown by computer programming of game theories that a game called Tit for Tat eventually leads to advantageous cooperation. In the Tit for Tat computer program players return only what has been given to them. One never initiates injuries or makes the first harmful move, but one always returns in equal measure an injury that has been given. Following this systematic program the eventual outcome of the game is cooperation and a condition of mutual advantage. This computer model has been used as evidence to explain the evolution of cooperation in everything from animal to human organisms.

So why does Christianity burden us with the impossible demand to forgive all injuries? This seems impossible to do if the common wisdom of the ages or our developed systems of justice can be believed. Is the command to forgive all injuries only to be followed by Christians as a supererogatory course for believers? Does it have any practical or common-sense justification as a way of life for ordinary people in our society?

For that matter, how can anyone succeed in this incredibly difficult task that goes so much against the grain?

We often do not have a clear idea of what forgiveness entails, nor do we think enough about how to do it. To struggle with these questions of why and how to forgive I will begin by reflecting on the why questions and work through to the how questions. Along the way I will focus on what injuries are, and what forgiveness is. Thinking about what hurts us and why it hurts, helps us grapple with what must be involved in acts of forgiveness.

WHY MUST CHRISTIANS FORGIVE ALL INJURIES?

The question of why we should forgive has pragmatic answers which will be addressed below, but the theological dimension of the question must also be considered. For Christians there is simply no escaping God's demand that we forgive injuries. While the Old Testament's message about forgiving and holding no grudges, may be seen as ambivalent when placed alongside of biblical accounts of divinely approved vengeance, Christianity makes forgiveness of injuries a clear commandment for a follower of Jesus Christ. We must forgive injuries because God has forgiven us and we are commanded to be holy and perfect as God is perfect. Christians must forgive injuries because Jesus has testified in word and deed to the ultimate importance of God's demand that we forgive our enemies. In saying after saying, parable after parable, command after command, Jesus reiterates the demand summed up in the Lord's Prayer that we must forgive those who trespass against us.

Paul's letters, the rest of Scripture, and the testimony of the saints, martyrs, and mystics instruct and reinstruct Christians to forgive, to love their enemies, to return good for evil. Naturally this Christian teaching has always been a great stumbling block, a perpetual offense to good pagan common sense. Clearly, the Christian faith comes with this demand, a command that cannot be avoided, reinterpreted, or demythologized. This command points to the strait gate, the narrow way. Hard and unnatural as it is, forgiveness seems to be at the heart of the Gospel. Obeying this command to return good for evil must clearly differentiate the followers of Jesus: Christians, to be Christians, must freely forgive all injuries.

We must forgive all those who injure us, but worst of all, we must forgive those who continue to persecute us with no show of repentance. We must forgive those who are not about to ask our forgiveness. Christian forgiveness does not wait upon the enemy's repentance or request for restored relations. Of course it is wonderful if through repentance, interpersonal peace and community is restored. But the Gospel demand seems clear. Often forgiveness must be unilateral and a one-way process. We are told to forgive our injuries, even though the other person does not deserve it, is not sorry, and has not asked to be forgiven. Indeed many of the people that we have to struggle to forgive are those who have injured us in the distant past. Such persons are either no longer available or even alive, so they can be forgiven only unilaterally. Since injuries inflicted and hurts delivered can linger long after the injurers have departed, forgiveness must often be a one-way process.

WHAT ARE THE INJURIES AND TRESPASSES AGAINST US?

What constitutes an injury we are commanded to forgive, and what counts as a trespass against us? How do you hurt me? Let me count the ways. Injuries come in all varieties. But a real injury is rarely physical, nor does it come by accident.

The essence of an injury inheres in the negative psychological intention or motivation on the part of the injurer. Intended malice or evil directed toward our person produces the real injury, whether anything physical is involved. An accident, which by definition is not intended, can be fairly neutral in our psychological life—as long as it is not the result of criminal negligence or reckless self-indulgence. Accidents, along with natural disasters, can be seen more as misfortunes, or as the residual evil of disorder and chaos of the world; they are hardly injuries directed at us and calling for acts of forgiveness. If I am harmed by an earthquake or caught in a tornado, I am not offended or injured in a personal way. Real injuries are those acts that are aimed at us, as specific known persons, alive and operating in the world in this particular time and place. The perpetuators personally intended, or did not prevent when they could have, the particular harm inflicted upon us.

Our sense of injury increases in proportion to the amount of voluntary control and exercise of personal will that is involved in the harm. If someone carelessly falls asleep and causes us injury, even a great injury, this is of a different order from a case in which someone has plotted and connived to make us unhappy or to bring evil into our lives. Serious, freely enacted sins against us are the injuries that are most difficult to forgive. Of course, many people find it difficult to believe in sin, and therefore cannot accept that people could desire, plan, or carry out evil actions directed toward others. Some of these skeptics deny free will, or deny persons enough control over their lives to carry out malevolent projects, or deny that people could ever truly desire evil. Such doubters will stoutly maintain that there is no such thing as a deliberate injury aimed at another, necessitating personal acts of forgiveness.

Our concept of injury is inevitably related to our concept of the human potential for evil and sin. The idea of injury is also dependent upon an acceptance of the existence of a real self that can truly suffer. Those philosophies and religions that deny the reality of the self can also deny the reality of evil and treat personal injuries as simply another illusion. There can never be anything to forgive because there is no reality to the evil and suffering that is being falsely perceived. So, in a paradoxical sense, when one accepts the existence of injury and suffering as real phenomenona, it is an affirmation of the reality of the individual self that can suffer, and an affirmation of another individual's freedom and power to will evil. Accepting a divine savior's real suffering upon the cross validates our own human existence as nonillusory individual conscious selves who experience nonillusory suffering inflicted by nonillusory other selves intending to do us harm.

But how difficult it is for certain proud persons to accept the reality of their own personal injury and suffering. Strong characters are inevitably attracted to the stoic ideal of transcending all suffering through strength of will and superior detachment. To admit that they have been injured is a confession of weakness and vulnerability. It hurts to recognize that one is hurting, or that one is weak enough to be hurt by another. Trapped in their desire for omnipotence, a defense that perhaps begins in the child who has to use this strategy against suffering, proud persons can simply deny that they are being injured. They continue to maintain that nothing hurts and that no one has succeeded in penetrating the self's defenses to inflict harm or pain. No one can "get to me."

To recognize the pain and the injury is a necessary first step in being able to forgive. Sometimes the recognition of pain and injury is absolutely necessary for safety and future survival. Individuals can so deny injuries that they fail to take necessary steps to flee imminent danger. Bruno Bettelheim talks of the Jews of Nazi Germany in the 1930s who simply refused to recognize injury after injury; they could not accept the signs that so much evil was intentionally being directed toward them as a group. Their "pathology of hope" and denial of malice helped them eventually to perish. Women, too, have denied and excused the pain and injury of physical abuse by their husbands and have paid with their lives. Ironically, extremes of either arrogance or innocence can lead to dangerous denials of pain and injury.

Once one accepts the existence of injuries it is easy to see that injuries can come in many ways. Each of these varieties or categories necessitates different efforts and involves different capacities in order to forgive. One dimension of injury is how close it comes to the innermost being of a person. The self is experienced as a physical self and a social self and a spiritual self with many different facets. Each of these dimensions of the self can be injured in different ways. The more important the dimension attacked, or the closer to the center of the self, the more hurtful the injury will be. Injuries aimed at external nonessential parts of my life or being can quickly and easily be forgiven. Injuries to my deepest self, my sense of well-being, my self-esteem, my sense of honor and integrity, or my deepest commitments will hurt more and be much more difficult to forgive. The rather enigmatic saying of Jesus that he who calls a person a fool shall be in danger of hellfire, makes sense when one thinks of how much it hurts to be called a fool and have one's sense of self, or competence and worth, publicly insulted.

Since I invest my self in others, vicarious injuries also hurt. Since I identify so closely with those I love most in the world, injuries done to them are injuries done to me. Injuries done to one's beloved spouse or children or parents or friends may sometimes be more difficult to forgive than injuries that are done to one's self. This human propensity to take umbrage at the injury done to one's family and friends fuels the ongoing feuds and vendettas that have marred the world's history. One's communal honor, or group self-esteem, can also be injured by insult and indignities. Especially in traditional societies, group identification can be very strong. In some cases communal honor can be injured by shameful behavior on the part of a member of the group. Honor killings are committed in revenge for a betrayed group's shame.

Detraction or bearing false witness may be among the worst injuries because personal repute lives on in a community, residing for prolonged periods in the minds of others. To have one's good name or honor or integrity or virtue impugned among one's peers is a grievous injury. We are communal beings who live with others and are ever conscious of the fact that our character is considered by others. We seek social esteem far more than material goods. It would take almost superhuman detachment not to be hurt by a malicious attack on one's public reputation and character.

Another dimension in the categorizing of injuries is that of time. There can be one-time injuries that were done long ago and are over and done with. Then there are injuries that once initiated, continue on and become chronic problems. Another dimension of injury is the inducement of anxiety and dread—a favorite tactic of torturers. The onset of an injury in time also affects its quality. There can be slowly developing problems that are so obviously signaled that the eventual injury is expected. Then there can be totally unexpected and shocking injuries delivered out of the blue. The unexpected injury is difficult to bear because in addition to the injury itself, the victim has to deal with the shock and surprise of the attack or sudden betrayal. Sudden injury or betrayal is particularly traumatic because one's belief system is turned upside down. Rape victims, for instance, find the suddenness of the assault particularly upsetting, and the subsequent mistrust and anxiety are difficult to bear.

Who injures me is another crucial factor in injury. When an enemy or acquaintance or a distant colleague injures me, this does not have the impact of an injury done by someone I have loved and trusted. The more intimate the relationship, the more ideals and values are shared, the more the injury will hurt. The old saying that you always hurt the ones you love is true, because a love relationship makes a person more vulnerable to injury. The closer the injurer is, the more the injury and hurt is felt.

The most hurtful injury of all may be the betrayal of trust by a beloved person who has shared one's life. So marriage partners and family members and intimate friends can hurt each other more than anyone else. Next, perhaps, come comrades and those who have fought together and shared a mutual investment and struggle for a common cause. Civil wars and fighting among alienated political allies can be most bitter. We react so strongly when those who are close and beloved hurt us, because besides the hurt, we are forced to doubt our past life together. Has this person changed, or did I not really know him as I thought I did? Was I totally wrong in my estimation of his character and our relationship?

Perhaps the worst part of an injury from a beloved person is that it can penetrate our habitual defenses and diminish our innermost selves. If the person I love and identify with injures me, I am drawn into my own victimization through my intimate union with him or her. If you repudiate me, I inevitably begin to see myself through your eyes and feel diminished; I am not only hurt, but feel demeaned and maimed by the self-repudiation you have induced in me. When deep betrayals by beloved persons occur, a person can be nearly annihilated by the injury; the shared life, the mutual love, and all the ideals and values that have formed the committed bond of the past are trampled upon and called into question. Perhaps a completely self-confident, self-sufficient person would not be deeply injured or hurt in such a situation, but any person so invulnerable to hurt would also be detached from love and interdependency.

The fact that victims can be led into their own victimization produces the potential for all types of chronic abuse. Many abusers convince their victims that nothing wrong is happening. If anything seems to be the matter it is the victim's fault and the result of their own wrongdoing or weakness. Injury is compounded by the deceptive efforts to confuse, project blame, and keep the victim from escaping the psychological bind. A person's very sanity can be threatened when such subtle assaults are prolonged. Since people who sin usually project and protect their sin to avoid their own guilt, they can spend enormous energy blaming, persecuting, and attacking the person who is truly the victim. The need to escape guilt impels a persecutor to make the victims feel that their perception of reality is completely distorted. The injured victim is then not only betrayed but forced into destructive self-doubt and self-repudiation. Unfortunately, this kind of ensnaring evil takes place frequently in marriage and family life.

A dreadful injury takes place when a beloved spouse betrays his or her marital partner with infidelity. Such injuries are horrible because every level of one's being is betrayed. The belief in one's world is overturned, the trust that one is beloved and that one is the object of loyalty is destroyed. When betrayal is discovered suddenly and shockingly after much deception and the kind of lies that accompany such betrayals, the hurt is compounded. The sense of desperation, sorrow, hurt, and annihilation inflamed by jealousy and desire for revenge, produces an injury that is unique. The injured spouse cries out, "How could my beloved do this to me? Indeed, how could this person I trusted and admired do this at all?" Every dimension of self suffers, from sexual validation and self-respect, to one's commitment to promises and good faith.

The hurt and suffering brought about by infidelity in a marriage becomes almost overwhelming—and the better the marriage the worse it is. The sense of despair and pain is psychological, but soon can be manifest physically. Betrayed, bereft persons lose weight, become physically weak, or contract illnesses. A broken heart is not just symbolic. The common experience of human beings in every age validates this symbol of deep injury as that most difficult to forgive. One can see why this image of the betrayed spouse was used in the Old Testament as the ultimate injury and challenge to loving forgiveness. The people of Israel are depicted as the unfaithful spouse of the Lord; the people sin and yet receive God's free forgiveness. It is far easier to understand injury than it is to understand forgiveness.

FORGIVENESS

What exactly is meant by forgiveness? What do we do when we forgive the sinner? It is ironic that millions of Christians every day pray for forgiveness and speak of forgiving trespasses, yet are not quite sure exactly what is involved. Is to forgive to totally forget the injury, or is it to so understand that one excuses the injury? Before going on to discuss how one can manage the act of forgiving injuries, it would be well to know what it is one is aiming for. When we are told to forgive one another as God has forgiven us we need a more distinct concept or sharper focus upon what it is we are about to attempt.

Since injury is a phenomenon of many dimensions it may be that forgiveness is equally complex. There are different levels and types of forgiveness with differing developments and courses. There are times when one has been able to forgive on a very rational symbolic level, but has not really, truly, deeply forgiven with one's whole being. Without the emotional follow-through the forgiveness remains at a superficial level. Sometimes the symbolic cognitive forgiveness only initiates the long process that will finally result in full and complete forgiveness. A happier discontinuity can also be experienced when one finds that one has already forgiven on a deep emotional level when at a conscious verbal level one did not know one was yet able to do so. People sometimes find themselves mysteriously making up, long before they thought they could be ready.

One can guess that those people who have a hard time accepting that they have been injured are the same people who have trouble forgiving from the heart. They habitually operate on a very rational level quite removed from the deep springs of their personality. They are too proud to admit injury, but when forced to do so they use the same pride to forgive—on a certain level. Their forgiveness serves an aggressive need to dominate by being morally superior. The high tone of the person too willing to forgive an injury too lightly felt, has an artificial and disquieting effect. A full, deep act of forgiveness can only come after a full acceptance of how hurt one has been, and how the injury has taken its toll. One has to go down deep into the injury and accept the full measure of pain before one can truly begin to forgive.

Does true forgiveness mean that one finally forgets the injury? A friend whose spiritual judgment I respect says with absolute certainty that "to forgive is to forget," indeed, it is the only way that one can truly forgive another. Many others champion this amnesiac approach to forgiveness. But the idea of equating forgetting with forgiving doesn't work. It is too simple. After all, my memory, my consciousness of existing through time, my personal history, must necessarily be maintained as a part of my present identity, my present self. Therefore I cannot simply blot out sections of my past or painful episodes and still retain all that I have been, which is the foundation for all that I have become today. The past cannot be denied or undone. If we use our defenses to seal over past problems with denial or repression rather than facing up to the painful reality, we incur another psychic cost. I think direct confrontation and working through what happened is the better way to forgiveness.

In this world, time is irreversible; it flows in only one

direction. An injury, even a long-ago injury, much less one that is recent or chronically present, cannot simply be erased from one's personal history. Something much more complicated than amnesia has to be effected in an act of forgiveness. But what? Is perhaps the better way a deliberate strategy of minimizing through an effort to explain away the injury? Knowing that to err is human, many would hold that to understand all, is to forgive all. In this understanding approach, one basically equates forgiving with excusing. If only one could understand how insecure the person who injured you was, how deprived, how stressed, how handicapped by upbringing, and so on, and so on. A true understanding all of the relevant factors and variables will lead one to see how what happened at that particular time came to be—indeed, given all the variables, was practically inevitable.

Unfortunately, the excusatory environmental approach takes away moral responsibility from a person. In the process of explaining evil acts through some soft social determinism, it explains away freedom and choice on the part of the person who injures, and, by implication, my own moral responsibility. Why or how, then, can I be expected to have enough freedom to forgive an injury? Admittedly, at times some people do act involuntarily and are not in control of their actions. But it is also true that many human choices remain in every situation, and that the past free choices of a person have helped shape their present situation. In many cases, persons freely choose to harm one another. Their evil intent may be far greater than the harm they succeed in doing. Explanations may occasionally be a road to forgiveness but they can never be the whole story. To forgive someone who knows not what they do is one thing. To forgive someone who knows very well what they are doing, and does it anyway, is the real challenge.

Forgiving, then, is neither forgetting, nor excusing. The reality of the injury remains in memory. Its seriousness and the actual evil intent is neither denied nor excused in some misguided effort to deny the reality of sin and free will. But the past reality must now be transformed in the present by a free act of love and forgiveness. Forgiveness essentially means restoring one's relationships to wholeness, giving to another goodwill, love, and care, despite the other's efforts to rend the relationship. The reality of another's malice is not denied, but the inner personal reality of present goodwill and hope for a loving future transforms the past. God's love, which can remove the sting of death, can remove the sting and bitterness of a past injury. The memory of the wrongdoing and suffering remains intact but the anger and wrath or sorrow and despair of the past no longer accompanies the recollection.

After full forgiveness the memory of the injury is divested of its agonizing emotional component because the present emotions of goodwill or love or care or hope are stronger than the negative anguish that was experienced with the injury. It is as if the injury recedes far, far away in time, or shrinks in perspective in proportion to the whole picture. What was overwhelmingly in the foreground becomes another part of the background, the insistent searing quality of a still-throbbing injury fades into the overall design. The restoration of wholeness, as in physical healing, re-creates psychological networks, new patterns that overlay the gaping wound. Something that was broken is mended. The breach that seemed impossible to bridge is overcome.

Consider the worst case, the injury inflicted by the infidelity of a marriage partner. Here there is a betrayal of trust, with marriage vows and promises broken; moreover, lies, manipulation, and deceit usually accompany the rejection of the spouse. Such treatment hurts horribly, especially if it is accompanied by hostility. Often a guilty party will try to justify his or her actions by attacking the innocent spouse in a classic case of blaming the victim or scapegoating. After such breaches of trust, forgiveness requires an inner healing of the wounds. The betrayed spouse must be restored to self-esteem and wholeness, if he or she is to begin to see the injury and injurer differently. If repentance is sought and the guilty person wishes to be forgiven and to continue the marriage, the restoration of the breach will mean rebuilding together. To do this, the marital love that exists in the present and can continue to exist in the future, will have to seem more of a reality than the past betrayal and injury. With forgiveness, the past no longer poisons the present or future relationship. While the past can never be undone, forgotten, or explained away, it will no longer call the tune for the present relationship. Forgiveness restores goodwill, friendship, and loving hope; positive emotions are dominant in the mind and heart of the wronged person.

When forgiveness occurs, the present and the future dominate the inner stream of consciousness. Loving concern reigns, instead of despair, hurt, bitterness, or wrath. If actual mutuality is restored and the partner is back in the relationship, then each day's action can demonstrate the new focus. Resurrections of marital relationships are possible.

There are some very sorrowful cases in which an injured person may have to separate himself or herself from an unrepentant chronic abuser. Often separation is necessary for physical or psychological survival. In any event, forgiveness must be achieved if the victim is to survive and grow. The restoration of wholeness will still involve a transformation of attitude toward the other, now absent, partner. Past injuries must be worked through and emotionally resolved, even if the other person refuses to cooperate. Let the dead bury the dead. A person who forgives is interested in love and life now. There just isn't enough psychological energy left for bitterness, or enough time left to be wasted on wrath.

Our knowledge of forgiveness comes from understanding how God forgives us our sins and repeated failings. God forgives us, though our sins be scarlet they shall be white as snow. The whole imagery of washing and whitening implies the transformation and restoration possible through God's saving love for us. Jesus, through his healing actions and teaching, confirms in our hearts and minds God's love and forgiveness to the sinner. Most important is the Resurrection and the coming of the new Jerusalem and the marriage of the Lamb. God is a God who makes all things new, a God of love with the power to transform the past into a redeemed present, full of abundant future. We are to love in the same re-creating way. Yes, love always means being sorry and asking forgiveness, but receiving forgiveness also means caring and wanting the best for the other person. One actively desires to see the other flourish. The essence of love is harmony, communion, joy, and attention to the happiness of the beloved.

God transforms us and the world through love and forgiveness. The God of power and might seems intent on the ultimate victory embodied in the restoration of loving relationships. Forgiveness is the only means to make this marriage feast of reconciliation happen. Imitating God, the loving person forgives; he or she is even unbecomingly excessive in eagerness to forgive and restore the broken bond. In Jesus' story of the father and the prodigal son, the father sees his son from afar and runs to meet him. The feasting and joy that mark true forgiveness, from finding lost sheep to lost children, are perennial themes in the Gospel good news. Our hearts burn within us when we hear these stories because we have known the joy of forgiving and being forgiven, the joy of reconciliation.

The ultimate exemplary model for our forgiveness can be found in Jesus' forgiveness of those who crucified him, freely given while in the midst of agony and pain. The magnanimity and large-heartedness of this ability to forgive inspires us to do the same. Nothing that we sinners suffer can be harder to forgive than what Jesus clearly forgives at that moment of torture and death. One wonders if this supreme act of forgiveness includes those acts that Jesus seemed to have had a harder time forgiving during his ministry. His words about those who have misled the little ones, or hypocritically put burdens upon the already burdened, or made life more difficult for the poor, seem to confirm that forgiving those who hurt those who are dear to us is a most difficult task.

Forgiving those who injure me may be easier than forgiving those who injure my child. But yet we must forgive, and transform all relationships that have been broken. If not, the cycle of vengeance and retribution goes on forever. Evil triumphs in acts of continued vengeance, as demonstrated by the deforming hate in the Middle East or Northern Ireland. We must not only do good to those who injure us but also to those who injure those we love. This is what we mean by "going the second mile." This is truly obeying and imitating God who gives goodness to the just and injust. Ironically, our consciousness and ability to remember, which is basic to our human identity, makes it harder for us to forgive. Caught as we are in resurgent memories and anger, we need help in our efforts to forgive.

HOW TO FORGIVE ALL INJURIES

Our knowing that we must forgive injuries doesn't make it any easier to do. In fact, forgiving injuries is perhaps the hardest thing that we will ever have to do, the severest test of our Christian commitment. The difficulty of this ordinary challenge of everyday life surprises us. Given what we know of the horrors of modern warfare, many of us might imagine that the ultimate test of our faith and character would be whether we could stand up under torture or behave with dignity in a concentration camp. Yet as we pass into middle-class American middle age, it seems unlikely that we will ever be tortured or have to face incarceration in a camp or totalitarian prison. For us, as it turns out, forgiving those who injure us becomes the most difficult test of our faith and character.

Forgiving all injuries is so completely against our human nature that we give up in despair and recognize that we are unable to do it by ourselves. We simply can't do it without God. The strength of our evil desire for vengeance is, for many of us, the most convincing evidence we have experienced firsthand of the human need for God's grace in order to avoid evil and do good. Only God's power and Christ in us can help us to restrain ourselves from evil and truly forgive. We may never have known how pagan and unconverted our hearts really were, until faced with a grievous wrong done to us. Then bitterness, anger, despair, and the desire for revenge rise up like a tidal wave and threaten to overwhelm us. The assault of these waves of bitterness and wrath and sorrow and pain are all but overwhelming. One can almost feel oneself being pulled down and beginning to drown in pain and fury and plans for revenge.

Once one sinks into this state it is a long time before one can rise to the surface again. But as one begins to go down sometimes the descent can be averted by the fervent invocation: "Jesus Christ, liberator, save me from this madness, pain, and hate." If the invocation is given too late and one sinks anyway, then all that can be done is to try to remember Jesus Christ crucified and hope that one's self-control can at least keep one from doing anything more overtly evil than succumbing to one's inner rages of vindictiveness and wrath. God can at least keep one from drowning in the confusion and evil as the inner storm batters on. No wonder the anchor was an early symbol of Jesus Christ. It is also understandable that Christians considered these losses of control and overwhelming desires to do evil to be temptations by the Devil. One can almost feel oneself being seduced into evil and feel the temptation to give way to pain and anger. How delighted Satan (if he exists) must be with these falls into wrath and bitterness.

Not only has evil been done by the injurer, but the victim is also ensnared in evil desires, with ensuing bouts of distress and self-loathing.

Not to forgive injuries is hell. To carry the anger, wrath, pain, and distress that accompany a sense of injury is to remain in confused chaotic turmoil. One flails and writhes in pain and hate, feeling tortured, torn apart, and impotent. An odd conflict can arise for the good person who is caught in a peculiar bind. A person can know that they could never let themselves exact vengeance, yet they still lust to inflict punishment upon their tormentors. It is even more galling to realize that a wrongdoer may escape retribution within one's power because it would be a greater evil for one to seek revenge. Good persons can be trapped by their own strength of character and self-control, too obedient in conscience to take revenge, but not Christlike enough not to want to. After experiencing such divided and tormented states, a Christian can give ready assent to the truth that all the way to hell is hell.

Experience gradually convinces us that God's commands are always for our good; Christ's yoke is light indeed compared to the burdens of evil. Undergirding the commands of faith and duty, there exists a moral reality that arises from the psychological laws of our human nature. From a purely secular point of view, it is important to be able to forgive our injurers for the sake of our own health and happiness. The stress and turmoil of bitter anger is bad for the heart, both literally and figuratively. When one cannot or will not forgive an injury one remains in the position of battered and bitter victim, constantly aroused and hurting, constantly impaired, constantly maimed, because one is constantly conscious of the injury as it dominates and permeates the present. Nursing one's anger and nestling down into injury guarantees the victimized condition, the defeated state of weakness and pain. How can one escape? How can one be liberated?

When one enacts a spiritual work of mercy or tries to love another, a threefold attention must take place: one must attend to one's relationship to God, to one's relationship to others, and to one's inner self. Wherever one begins, one must get around to the other factors before things can change decisively. To forgive an injury one can begin with a cry to God for help. Faced with one's failure to be able to love and forgive, one is driven to faith. Only God's love is stronger than hate, stronger than anger, stronger than natural pride and the desire for vengeance. With God nothing is impossible. Through faith I can hope that I can be healed. If Jesus Christ rose from the dead and conquered death and hate, Christ in me can conquer this living death. In misery I long for the peace of Christ which comes through forgiveness—for me, for my enemy, for us.

But as in all psychological struggles for control, a curious condition is recognized in both theology and secular psychology. The more one struggles to conquer and fight an evil urge, the less one is able to do it. Psychologists talk about the law of least effort in which one is best able to change or to direct consciousness through the most minimal effort needed. Large-scale frontal assaults provoke reactions and defensiveness and thereby are more likely to fail. The image used in illustration is that of the swimmer who only by gently floating above the incoming wave can surmount it successfully; the person who fights the wave head on is knocked down, bruised, and perhaps even drowned.

The paradoxical psychological process seems to work because measures of attack provoke countermeasures of resistance. In addition, as one struggles to control evil, attention is focused upon the temptation or evil desire or habit, and such an attentive focus magnifies and strengthens its object. If, by contrast, attention can be directed elsewhere and a quiet sense of trust and confidence can be maintained, a person can gently float over or bypass the obsessive problem. Ironically, giving up the struggle and turning to a higher power in trust, can achieve what a determined effort cannot. Many self-help movements, beginning with Alcoholics Anonymous, make giving up and turning one's life over to a higher power the first step in regaining power to change. It is almost a secular version of justification by faith.

When my trust is focused upon God's power as the ultimate source of energy in the creation then I believe I can be transformed by Christ within me. God and Christ and the Holy Spirit within can empower me to forgiveness of an injury that would otherwise be impossible. I must let go and ask God to heal me, an act which is very difficult for strong, self-sufficient persons. Attending to God one tries to identify with God's point of view. Thinking of God's goodness we inevitably recognize that we, too, are sinners and have injured others. We ask forgiveness for our own trespasses. Realizing our own sins and injuries delivered to others gives us some sense of fellow feeling with the person who has injured us. Going to confession more frequently helps in this process. My enemy is not the only perpetuator of evil; we both share this ability to hurt. (In some cases we may have even hurt our present injurer in the past, a circumstance that can make present forgiveness somewhat easier.) Thinking God's thoughts we must also remember that this person who has injured us also has Christ within, and is also one of the beloved children of God. We may begin to look at them and then feel toward them the way God must feel toward them; we pity them and feel sorry for their sake. How sad that they have erred and strayed and offended God and their better selves! It is hard to feel sadness and hate at the same time. With much prayer, sadness may triumph over our anger.

Of course, change toward another cannot happen without a revolution of one's own inner life. An inner transformation must accompany the transformation of the relationship with others. The reconciliation with another that is desired has to begin with an inner reconciliation. The injury, hurt, and sorrow, have to be overcome with an inner healing. After all, the injury has made one feel hurt, repudiated, attacked, and lowered in self-esteem. The vulnerability and weakness that we all have, have been touched and we have been trampled on in some way. In the condition of turmoil to which the injurer has brought us, we cannot be free to rise above our bitterness or feel strong enough to love. We have been hated and deeply hurt, half-convinced of our enemy's scorn and repudiating acts. Our self-esteem may be nearly in shreds.

In such times of agony and conflict, we can truly cry out the words of the Psalmist (words which may have seemed excessive before we needed them): "Oh, God, my God, come to my rescue, comfort me in my affliction, do not let me be put to shame in the presence of my enemies." It is imperative that we begin to look at ourselves as the beloved child of God. We must give real assent to the reality that God loves us and wishes to comfort us, and will do so if we can open ourselves up to His love. The Great and Holy One will rescue us from this evil.

We need to dwell again and again on the Gospel words of love and assurance to help ourselves believe that God really and truly does love us so much. The sacrament of the Mass helps us believe. Slowly one can begin to feel whole again. One forgives oneself for feeling anger and indignation and desire for vengeance, realizing that while this is sin it arises from part of our nature, a part which in appropriate circumstances helps fuel the thirst for justice. Forgiving ourselves and beginning to see ourselves as loved by God, also begins to repair the damage that has been done to us. The most hurtful things happen when we have believed what the person who injured us has tried to tell us by their injury—that we are inferior, that we are unworthy of good treatment, that we are nothing. Beginning to feel loved we can begin to trust ourselves, to have self-confidence, and to trust others enough so that we can begin to forgive. We look at others as we do ourselves; in forgiveness we can look at self and others in a benign way. Then we are truly healed and whole and re-collected, once more at peace.

We regain our peace, our sense of wholeness, our sense of self-love and love for others by taking God's point of view and asking God to help us love ourselves and others as He loves. But achieving this reconciliation may be a long and difficult process with many complexities. Just as injury is complex, so is forgiveness. Time and repeated efforts may be necessary. Bitterness may come in cycles and surge up again and again. Perseverance in forgiveness is necessary so that the new trans-formed peaceful self becomes permanent. There is usually an acute phase of suffering after an injury and then the immedi-ate shock and trauma give way to a longer more chronic cyclical condition. Different strategies may be appropriate at different times. A full immersion and catharsis in hurt may seem less appropriate as time passes and the upsurges of anger and hurt become less frequent and less powerful and potent. A simple dismissal and affirmation may work. As grief and mourning have its phases so do acts of forgiveness. The capacity to love and forgive can become more fully and com-pletely a part of our life.

In a sense our life as it progresses is a continual process of forgiving past injuries. As one grows older one can begin to forgive the past injuries that have been done to almost all children by almost every parent. Since we are all sinners, in every life there have been injuries in the past that need to be healed in order to achieve present and future wholeness. Even if the people are no longer present the healing process of forgiveness needs to be carried out. In certain cases where real injuries are continuously present this process is much more difficult and becomes a case of bearing wrongs patiently. If old injuries are not forgiven they have a horrible way of being repeated in one's own life as though some unconscious programming has been laid down to be followed in the future, even to the next generation.

Life is full of forgiveness and in a sense we become better at it as we learn to love more deeply and more fully through deeper responses to God's love for us. Gradually we learn to let go more and more of our past injuries, hates, and troubles, which have knotted us up and depleted energy from the present and the future. We become more liberated from all injury and inferiority and know joy and peace. To forgive is to be forgiven, to be forgiven empowers forgiveness; love begets mercy and mercy begets more love.

7

TO PRAY FOR THE LIVING AND THE DEAD

Pray all the time, asking for what you need, praying in the Spirit on every possible occasion. Never get tired of staying awake to pray for all the saints; and pray for me. (Ephesians 6:18)

We are quite confident that if we ask him for anything, and it is in accordance with his will, he will hear us. (John 5:9)

There is no need to worry; but if there is anything you need, pray for it, asking God for it with prayer and thanksgiving. (Philippians 4:6)

QUESTIONS ABOUT PRAYER

We have been told to pray and we have the example of Jesus and the saints and the Church constantly before us. We have experienced the power of prayer in our lives and so continue to pray on pragmatic grounds as well as through faith. But do we understand what is happening? Reconsidering prayer and attempting to understand why and how this is a work of mercy will help us persevere. If we do not have an image or an insight into what we are doing it is more difficult to believe in our activity and keep doing it day after day. We need a better intuition of how prayer works, a clearer approximation of what happens. Traditionally, Christians have prayed for themselves, for others, and for the dead, but what does this mean in a world no longer tidily divided into earth, purgatory, heaven, and hell? Hard questions abound and induce new struggles to understand how prayer can make a difference.

I will start with some reflections on the case of personal petition and then move to the more difficult problems of praying for others, first the living and then the dead. Problems with prayer, especially the effectiveness of intercessory prayer, bring us to central questions about how God relates to the created order. How can there be divine interventions in a lawfully created universe? We know that the redemptive victory has been won by Jesus but that final battles continue in this time before the end. We live in an interim time described as "already but not yet." We believe that at the Creation God set the stage for our drama and that he has determined the finale of the script, but the middle acts seem to be open to the co-authorship of God and humankind. (Theological arguments turn on just how much human improvisation is demanded.) In any event, human beings are responsible for the dominion, stewardship, and exercise of freedom we have been given. God wins, we know, but *how* that victory of love will be consumated depends upon our human acts in this time of "not yet." Indeed, the whole Creation is groaning in the birth process of the Kingdom.

Those of us who have children of our own can begin to understand why God chooses to limit His divine power for the sake of human development. Parents do not wish to give their children only ready-made passive pleasures, but desire rather to enable their children to participate in the greater human pleasure of creating, achieving, growing, and developing through their own initiative and activity. Parents have to "let go" to give their children growing room for their own developmental struggle. Similarly, one of the greatest joys of being God must be the divine creativity, having the loving power to bring lives and worlds into being; so surely God desires similar creative joys for the beloved human beings made in the divine image. As Paul says, "we are God's work of art." Jesus has told us that we shall do greater works than he in Jesus' name; he has called us to be friends and join in the redemption of the world.

But to be truly creative and able to produce our own works of art, our freedom must not be illusory. God does not coerce. So we are free, with all the potential for harm and good that freedom brings. The Creation, although good, is separate from God and not divine, though God sustains it and the Spirit penetrates throughout, especially in human beings and within the community of the Church. Human beings and the Church are not divine, although, as the mystics say, we are God-seeds and have the potential to grow into adulthood as God's people. Into this separation and simultaneous interpenetration, into this space between the already and the not yet, the free activity of prayer can move. But how does it make a difference?

PRAYING FOR OURSELVES—PRAYERS OF PETITION

Many books are written today to instruct the faithful in prayer. Recordings and films, complete with music for meditation, exist as part of the current renaissance in spirituality. Pastoral courses are offered in all the many different kinds of prayer in the Christian tradition as well as new ways to mine the ancient treasuries found in Eastern spirituality. There exist a variety of ways for any individual to pray. But it is clear that we also are praying collectively and never simply as isolated individuals. We are members of the Church and pray within and through the Church. Even if we are not taking part in a public liturgical worship service, we are members of Christ's body and our prayers rise as members of that community. We should take to heart Baron von Hügel's admonition that in praying it is important always to "realize you are but one of a countless number of souls, a countless number of stars." All over the globe throughout each minute of every day the Church is praying.

We are also told in Scripture that the Spirit and Jesus pray for us to the Father. This divine giving and receiving of love and communion within the Trinity is the model for our own communication in prayer. But if the Spirit prays for us and we participate in the prayer of our high priest Jesus, why pray individually and privately beyond communal worship and the Eucharist? If prayer is a fundamental disposition of our whole being turned toward God, does overt explicit individual prayer add anything? Yes, indeed; surely an individual response of prayer is also called for, since we are separate self-conscious individuals who are able to communicate privately with thought and word and deed at the same time that we are members of one another and of the Church. One is still an individual, while being a member of a family.

We would never want to be like those family members who never talk because they assume that the others must already know what they would say, so they see no reason to speak of love and gratitude. Love by its nature seeks expression and is increased by expression. Besides, prayer is a way of specifically lifting heart and mind to God in adoration, gratitude, and petition and then listening for God's response. In a unique individual life there must be time for specific individual communications devoted to particular concerns. We must listen for our own special whisperings from the Spirit in answer to our prayers. We also know that in the act of thinking and communicating and voicing things, we discover new things that we did not know we knew. The process of active communication with others gives us new access to ourselves as we communicate. When the other listener is the divine Other, our communication can be even more creative. Although God knows everything and all our thoughts in the future as well as the past, we don't. Voicing our prayers entrains new thoughts and new ideas, by directing our attention to God.

Psychologically the way prayers of petition seem to work to transform our lives is through the operation of attention. Attention is that light of our consciousness which we can focus at will. As William James and others have noted, the one ultimate act of freedom at man's disposal is his ability to "keep the selected idea uppermost." When we attend to God and the divine love and goodness and truth, we are drawn into joyful adoration and loving attachment. These states produce more prayerful attention and induce desires to imitate God and pursue God's will in our lives. Slowly we become transformed as our habits of attention and attachment inevitably shape our thoughts, feelings, and behavior. As we grow in love for God we are more and more assured of God's love for us and so begin to be able to love others better. God's love for us overflows in love for others.

Consciousness of the fact that God loves us creates more love for the self. Self-esteem grows from being esteemed by another, and what an Other we discover in God. The amazing good news gradually sinks in; truly we have been created, redeemed, and cared for so that every hair of our head is numbered. God really does love us dearly, more ardently than any other person or parent could. This raises our sense of self-worth, even as it makes us humbly grateful for such excessive benevolence. Through prayer we begin to value ourselves in a new way so that the intertwined relationships of self to self, self to God, and self to others become transformed. Great lovers of God become increasingly aware that God is in each person and so begin to love and attend to the Christ in others. Love multiplies in bountiful profusion.

In prayer, the direction of consciousness and thought and emotion and action toward God is a movement that infuses in us the energy of God. God's zest, God's spirit, and God's power can come to us when we ask to receive it. Prayer is the way we participate more fully in God as Reality. Prayer is the way we open ourselves to the divine and ask that we, too, may become hearts from whom living water flows. A prayerful person rises up like an eagle and has youth perpetually renewed. I have also found that human beings much given to prayer *look* different, despite their original physical endowments given in the genetic throw. There is something particularly light and clear around the eyes. I do not think this is just my imagination operating, because reliable new psychological research on facial expressions shows that emotions habitually displayed in the hundreds of facial muscles can, over time, shape the way a face looks. As Abraham Lincoln long ago noted, after forty a man is responsible for his face. Moses' face shone with light when he had talked with Yahweh, and to this day reflections of a similar shining seem to appear in God's friends.

Unfortunately, the opposite is also true, the light can go out of a face—and a life. If we do not pray we cut ourselves off from the vine and begin to wither in our power and capacity to love others. Sometimes we may think that we do not need prayer or our communion with God to function and to live in the world. But over the years, we and those who live around us see that the withering has begun. In middle age a person begins to reap what has been sown. Once the youthful ego has either obtained satisfaction or been deeply frustrated, we see that it was ego that kept us striving, even in supposedly doing good for others. Without private prayer persons can become cut off from the spiritual source of life. They are not living abundantly.

We also need corporate prayer of course, prayer with our community. Both kinds of prayer are needed to keep our liveliness, to keep our merriment, and to restore our joy as life inevitably begins to take its toll and grind us down. The Spirit within us needs infusion from the Spirit of God. We need that communion to bear fruit. Without prayer we dry up and

become dead before the body dies. The thirst that we think
we can quench through work, worldly success, and a busy life
with friends and family cannot be quenched by any other
means than by drinking at the fount of the living water.

As we go through the various trials and tribulations of life's
struggles we find our prayer life expands and changes according to our need and life situation. However, the basics for
many of us who pray remain simply, "help, help, help," and
"thank you, thank you, thank you." These cries of the heart
are, of course, supplemented by all the great formal prayers of
the Church, and especially by the great Our Father, which
Jesus taught. We also can pray the Scriptures and the Psalms.
Marian devotions help many of us pray, just as the prayers of
the great saints or other traditional prayers, such as the Jesus
prayer, work for different individuals. Today we also have
access to other mystical traditions, such as the prayer of quiet,
and centering prayer. As we learn more from Zen and Yoga we
can see that in the West we must recapture a sense of praying
through the body and the physical dimensions of what has
been identified as the core self. Breathing, prayer postures, and
bodily actions can be used in prayer. These insights from afar
help us reconsider in our own tradition those physical acts
used in devotion that heretofore have been rather conde-
scendingly relegated to the folk-religion aspect of Catholicism.

If we can pray with all of our bodily being then climbing a
holy mountain, lighting candles, or standing vigils can be acts
of prayer. New efforts to incorporate prayer into daily life may
evolve. A woman I know uses quilting as an act of prayer for
her father. This seems a modern equivalent to the ancient
process of painting on cave walls, which was considered a form
of prayer (drawing over earlier drawings did not really matter
since the process rather than the product was most important
in the act of worship). In many other eras repetitive rhythmic
recitations, such as mantras, chants, or rosaries, have been
used for prayer. It is difficult to find something truly new

when it comes to human beings seeking contact with their Maker. I go to a health club and finish the exercise routine in the steam room. I thought I had discovered in the steam room, with its all-enveloping warmth, a new place to pray; as the steam rises up, so do prayers. But then I found that certain American Indian tribes had created similar prayer rituals with steam huts, using hot water and rocks to invoke the spirits, cleanse themselves, and allow their prayers to rise with the steam. Probably those who pray in the hot tub or during television commercials or during car trips can also find ancient precedents for what they consider totally modern practices.

Certainly it is most natural to pray in surging moments of great physical joy and triumph and delight. It seems appropriate to praise God at moments of orgasm, or when giving birth. David danced naked before the Ark of the Lord as an act of exhultant worship, and we can understand his motive. I can remember a need for a Deborah-like song of victory when my first baby was born and I was wild with excitement and ecstasy. Such peak experiences or natural highs induce prayer just as do quieter times of nursing or other wonderful embodied moments of feasting and joy. Knowing that Creation is good and really believing it, we can see that prayer at such moments of physical love or pleasure is fitting. Those enchained in the old dualisms of matter and spirit cannot see the positive dimension of praying through the flesh; they understand only fasting and painful disciplines as ways to pray with the body. Asceticism works, but the prayer of embodied joy also magnifies the Lord.

All of the different ways of prayerfully communicating with God expand the self and keep us in touch with what we need to live the liberated life. Prayer is a fundamental orientation before it is a specific act, but the acts are important as one lays one's own concerns before the presence of God. The thing to remember is 'to pray often and as one can, not as one cannot.'

Many pray as they would speak to a friend quite informally. Others have more of a sense of awe and distance, and pray more formally. I think that many women, sensing God as Mother, pray in informal intimate ways. When one looks at the great female mystics, for instance Julian of Norwich, one sees that the homeliness of women's experience gives them an ability to capture and understand the homeliness and sweetness and graciousness of the way that God deals with us. When God becomes a friend, nothing is too small to bring to the divine comforter. The little way in prayer means that prayer can be constant, unceasingly leavening the details of life with the inner dialogue.

We know that the continued process of prayer psychologically transforms a person, but is its power limited to the subjective domain? Yes, prayer makes me different, but does it make a difference otherwise? Can prayer transform reality beyond its influence upon the individual? The question of whether, or how, the petitions of prayer can intervene and change things or change others is a difficult one. Jesus prayed privately and personally but he also raised the dead, healed the sick, and successfully prayed for Peter's salvation, telling his followers to imitate him in their own faith and good works. Great saints comply and religious orders devote their lives to intercessory prayer, but we in the ordinary secular scientific world have difficulty grasping how to go about acts of intervention. Our problem is moving from the more easily explained subjective effects of prayer to understanding the effects of prayer in the objective world of matter and other people.

PRAYING FOR THE LIVING—INTERVENTIONS IN CREATION

The easiest thing to accept about intercessory prayer is that as in the case of praying for oneself, prayer will change the person who prays. Praying for another, especially an enemy, changes one's own attitudes and consequent behavior. When we pray for others we recognize them as fellow creatures beloved by God, and so we must seek God's will for them as well as for ourselves. This realization immediately transforms the way we attend to other persons. When we take a God's-eye view we have to enlarge our own narrow perspective and break out of the egocentric point of view. The distant and longer view immediately changes our attitude. If someone has hurt us or is an enemy and we wish to seek revenge, then prayer for them will eventually quiet our fury and dissolve our resentment. We cannot hold on to our enmity and at the same time pray that God's love should be in those who hurt us. Prayer creates a reconciliation and realignment in the subjective relationship we have with others.

Our prayers for those with whom we have a positive relationship loosen our needs to control or have others act as we will them to act (for their own good, of course). We give them into God's hands and so give up our obsessive anxiety over their welfare, a repetitive stabbing of sorrow that can destroy all composure and ability to think and act productively. To pray for another is to be healed and to be made whole, to come to a deep peace in one's subjective attitude. Experience shows us that praying for others works for us. Prayer heals, reconciles, changes, and enlarges our perspective toward them. Prayer reinforces the belief that another possesses dignity as a child of God; they are fellow family members with us in the human community. Our mutual dependence and our mutual origin in God's love and purpose are made manifest to us when we pray for these others. And the change in attitude bears fruit in changed behavior.

This changing and enlarging of perspective also works, of course, in the collective prayers of the Church when we pray in the liturgy of the Mass. We are moved out of ourselves into a more spacious, gracious, and beauty-filled world of love and truth. We come up from the gloomy confinement of our desires or despairs or detestations into the enormous vistas of God's perspective. The alternative reality gives us rest.

When we pray for others we help ourselves immensely, but can we be helping them? At the very least when we pray for others we create a network, a community of concern, a reaching out to others in a way that symbolically connects us in the minds of those in the community who are praying together. Consciousness, both individual and collective, is certainly being changed in a real way and will predispose us to different actions in future encounters. Yes, prayer can change another through my changed behavior toward them in direct encounters, but the problem is whether change can take place at a distance.

Changing the collective consciousness could affect an object of prayer only if there are interconnections between all persons and objects in the universe and if the heretofore understood physical laws of the universe are not immutable in their operations. Since faith is informed by reason and grace builds upon nature so it is instructive to look at the present state of the question in our present knowledge of nature. How connected are people? With the growth of the science of genetics we understand that we are all connected in our species membership, our common DNA going back to our earliest origins as a human group. There appears to be a common ancestry for all human beings so that we are all members of one another in sharing our genetic heritage. We can also see that as a species we share certain mental and bodily structures that result in common developmental patterns.

Perhaps most important is the new evidence that individual infants develop a sense of self and self-consciousness in orderly patterned ways that result from innate programs and early social nurturing. Studies of infants show that from the earliest experiences of being cared for, each infant seeks to orient and order reality and also seems to produce a gener-alized "evoked companion" who becomes incorporated into the human personality. This evoked companion, of course, invokes in a religious person thoughts of Jesus and the Spirit within, but in the eyes of child psychologists it is seen as the self-governing "significant other" or "generalized other" whose social response gives a child a maturing sense of self and individuality. We are all innately social as the self is created. We are "selved," to use Gerard Manley Hopkins's phrase, in wondrous ways from the very beginning. In a sense we do create ourselves as a human species, in physical pro-creation, in social ways as we evoke the affective self, and finally in cognitive and symbolic ways as we share language and rational communication. The idea that we exist as a com-mon human family has strong rational support. The belief in a universal human nature has had a resurgence in recent de-cades.

Psychologically, each of us is a member of the family and group that has created us, starting from the mother-child bond, and growing to include the father, the nuclear family, the kinship group, the community, the neighborhood, the linguistic-cultural group, and so on. By thinking the same thoughts in the same way and sharing feelings and actions we do have within ourselves all the persons who have influenced us psychologically and socially. As William James and Gordon Allport and other great psychologists say, we are socially a part of many other persons' lives and they are a part of ours. The social self always consists of others through the inner dialogue and imagined audience. But this communal consciousness, as far as we can ascertain, still resides within the body, skin, and brain of the individual person. While followers of a psycholo-gist like Jung have posited a collective unconscious, and others have insisted that links between individual con-sciousnesses exist, the evidence is not yet convincing enough for a skeptic to accept.

Psychologists have tried to prove that telepathy does exist and that communication can occur between persons at a distance. So far the evidence suggests no more than chance occurrences. Yet almost every person has had experiences of remarkable coincidences in which some contact seemed to be coming into the individual consciousness from a distant person. Religious traditions witness to such phenomena. Family members, lovers, and twins regularly claim such experiences. But the problem is whether these experiences are just examples of what has been called illusory correlation, in which two events seem related when they really are not. Our human perception and memory is so biased that we remember hits and successful incidents and often fail to take account of all the times when we are mistaken, or have intuitions that are not later confirmed. Believers in ESP retort with the observation that such experiences would, of course, be too particular and personal to be captured within the confines of scientific method.

But direct face-to-face social influence is incontestable. Social psychology has experimentally demonstrated group phenomena such as emotional contagion, mood shifts, conformity, norm setting, obedience, attitude shifts, stress reduction, and suggestion, to name only a few. Since communication can take place through many channels beyond words, the social influence of other persons in the environment is a powerful force. Human beings are always mutually influencing others in interesting systematic ways. Social rituals, rules, and signals given and received, constantly affect behavior even if we are not conscious of these nonverbal interactions. Social systems exist beyond individuals and role expectations can shape individual behavior. Families are now seen as small social systems with smaller social microenvironments within them. The systems approach to intervention and change is established: the presence of others and groups of others does affect us.

New understandings of the influence that others can have upon us in direct interaction can help explain the form of face-to-face intercessory prayer known as mediation. When a person is being prayed for in the presence of another or others, there can be effects socially conveyed in the same ways other group influence can be exerted. This influence may be particularly potent if there is physical contact. In the newest nursing research, and in behavioral medicine, there is an interest in investigating the operation of what is called "therapeutic touch." The role of touch, perhaps correlated with relaxation responses, hypnotic suggestion, and stress reduction, has proven effects. In traditional religious practice there has always been an emphasis upon prayer along with the laying on of hands, anointing, and healing touch. As science examines the mysterious workings of social influence and the relation of the body and immune system to other aspects of the person, the reported effects of direct face-to-face intercessory prayer do not seem so alien.

Face-to-face intercessory prayer of mediation can be understood as an act of love and charity for another. This aspect of this spiritual work of mercy assumes that the other who is present has asked for the prayer and is receptive to its influence. A fellow believer or believers can open themselves together to the transforming effects of prayer. But there is still the problem of intercessory prayer for those people or events at a distance. Suppose these persons are not believers, or don't know or don't care that they are being prayed for. Are they as removed from our interpersonal social influence as are, say, weather patterns or other parts of the natural world? In a way praying for rain and praying for persons at a distance present similar problems of intervention in the created order.

As regards praying for rain, when we think it absurd or impossible we are assuming that matter has its own immutable determined laws separate from human consciousness, and/or that God would not intervene in the lawful universe to change things for specific persons or events, since God loves all equally. Today, the old problem of matter and its lawfulness is being reconsidered by science. Old assumptions about the universe as a stably running machine with determined laws of cause and effect have vanished. While we still don't really know what matter or antimatter is, new respectable theories emphasize dynamic movement, relativity, openness, and the mysterious interconnections of all existing things. Elementary biology texts inform school children that every atom now in their bodies was once a part of the stars; humans living billions of years after the big bang are made of actual stardust. New theories of superstrings as the way matter is organized are even more amazing, for they emphasize anew how dense and interconnected all things in the universe are.

If matter is a form of active energy it makes sense to hypothesize that matter cannot be totally different from consciousness or mind that can activate the brain's energy fields. While we don't understand the whole picture, the universe seems to be differentiated by how fast the energy of things is changing. Everything is energy and everything is constantly changing, but some things appear solid to us simply because their rate of change is so much slower than our own. Even the earth is not solid but seething and bubbling at its core; rocks and bones and buildings look permanent to us because they change more slowly than soap bubbles. Computers compute like lightning because they use electricity, but their hardware also changes and will eventually decay. So far, in brain research it appears that our thoughts and consciousness are more like lightning, but with the involvement of the body's biochemistry far more complex than any computer.

With new research scientists can see the change in magnetic fields within the brain when attention is deployed in various ways. When told to pay attention to a song and ignore another concurrent stimuli one can detect a visible amplification of the electrical signals in the appropriate site in the brain—this demonstrates the human freedom to keep a selected idea uppermost. In other new research we see superconductors effecting magnetic fields so that heavy objects hover above a surface, as superconductive railroads will soon enable passenger trains to do. (Traditional reports of saintly levitation or walking on water do not seem so absurd when we have seen objects levitating in the lab.) It is not beyond reason to hypothesize that in a universe which seems to consist of electrical energy, the energy of directed human consciousness might be a force that could intervene in the energy patterns of matter. Russian psychological research has long been attempting to scientifically prove such telekinesis or direct influence of mind on matter. While all such attempts have so far been unsuccessful, such efforts, as in the equally unsuccessful efforts to provide conclusive evidence for ESP or telepathy, are not irrational.

Behavioral medicine has certainly concluded that human consciousness and emotional states affect the body's workings and have much to do in particular with the workings of the immune system. Just as we have always known that the body can affect the mind and brain, as in diseased and drugged states, we now know that causality can be a two-way path. As human individuals, we are self-conscious organic wholes made up of mind and body, always interacting with our environment in complicated ways. Our ultimate environment, the universe, increasingly seems to be a vast open changing system undergoing dynamic processes that are as yet poorly understood. Who knows to what destination Earth and the distant galaxies are hurtling through space, or what new forces or dimensions may exist beyond those we now know?

Instead of a giant machine, the universe seems better pictured as a dynamic, evolving open organism in which time itself is a relative dimension somehow interdependent with space. The thought that as we look out at distant galaxies we are looking at the youthful past of the universe boggles the mind. We can no longer look at time and matter in our old plodding way as fixed external constants. Laws of cause and effect must also be reconsidered and now the rational order of nature seems less deterministic and more like a varying range of patterns and probabilities. Influenced by evolutionary thinking, scientists emphasize the ways in which openness, chance, and change are built into patterns and events. There is both a lawful pattern and an openness in the processes of development that reveal themselves in the making of each unique snowflake as well as in the creation of each human personality, even perhaps in the earth as a self-regulating organism, or in the life and death of stars. Random chance and probabilities exist making various open combinations lawful and possible.

Such reflections about the universe must inform my intuitive understanding of intercessory prayer. To pray for rain or some other intervention in material events is not to pray for a complete overturning or contradiction of nature's laws. It can be better understood as an effort to affect or fix or focus the already open probabilities of the universe, which is constantly evolving and changing. Intercessory prayer at a distance when a person or group is facing some material confrontation—a drought, storm, disease, or journey—is an effort to ensure that certain benign combinations of probabilities take place rather than other possible combinations that may be destructive. The hope is that the energy of individual or group consciousness can interact with the energy inherent in matter so that chances and open probabilities in an evolving system can be affected for the good, through God's good grace.

The moral problem of why God would respond to specific requests or allow them to make a difference is also a difficult one. It seems that God has created a universe subject to law but that these laws include openness and change. We have been told in Scripture that in this "not yet" time before the Kingdom, the Creation, too, is groaning in its birth pangs, just as we are gradually being transformed or Christified. We have also been told to pray unceasingly for all things and to imitate Christ's works performed through intercessory prayer. Such struggle seems necessary because of the Fall: some wound in nature or the enslavement of Creation is evident, as we see evil prosper and the persistent reign of death and decay in our unjust, suffering world.

Perhaps, as in the parable, an enemy has sown weeds in the good fields of earth and we really do struggle, as Paul says, against spiritual forces of evil. It has long been argued whether a Devil or other fallen angels exist, or whether beliefs in personified evils are but symbolic ways of demonstrating the effects of the absence of good and of humanity's refusal of God's grace. Inertia and the absence of good, or the effective force of corrupted human abilities, can go a long way toward explaining human evil and suffering. But the demythologized explanations of evil do not account adequately for natural devastations, genetic accidents and disease, or the seemingly "demonic" violent outbreaks of collective human perversity and sadism. Whatever the origin of evil, a person who prays for others will have to confront evil ensconced in human actions and in natural forces and mischances.

There exists no fully satisfactory moral explanation of why, if God is all good and all powerful, so much evil and suffering suffuses the human condition. The only beginning we can make in accepting suffering is to see that the Creation is separate from God and that this separation is the condition of freedom necessary to achieve the separate identity of human beings who must live and grow in the limitations of time and space. The potential for evil is the price of our freedom. We have been given stewardship of the created world even though God permeates and sustains the universe in which we live and move and have our being. We can imagine that God is all around and throughout the Creation but separated and self-limiting enough so that separate human wills and actions will be free to make a real difference. God's noncoercive policy may mean that only human beings can freely invite and freely open their own human sphere to God's active power. God constantly broods over the Creation and is seeded within each human being. God longs to be invited to help. To ask is already to find. God is everywhere, but freely initiated human cooperation seems necessary to focus, activate, and magnify the divine force of love and power.

Prayer, especially intercessory prayer, may by its own god-given energy affect the world and at the same time directly infuse the universe with God's active love. Specific human requests in specific instances work because then God is invited into the human condition and separate creation, and the divine power can work overtly. The divine ground or horizon always sustains the whole creation, but specific events in our time and space are affected by free human acts and initiative. As human beings our every deed, thought, feeling, and prayer has its effect. The intercessory prayer of individuals and the Church may well be co-creating and co-redeeming the evolving universe. Teilhard de Chardin had such an understanding of human initiative, as have many poets and creative spirits. I love Annie Dillard's idea that each act of artistic creation and each act of ordering done by a human being, whether seen by another or not, helps create and sustain the universe. Convincing images of intercessory prayer contribute to our perseverance in prayer.

In Scripture we have been given many images of prayer. There is the familiar image of a child making requests from a loving parent or the other way around, as in the case of Mary at Cana. Other interpersonal images of intercessory prayer are those of the beseeching beggar, or the request for a superior authority's command (as in the case of the centurion). Prayers are also pictured as incense ascending or voices raised on high. For us today, nonverbal images of the operation of intercessory prayer are perhaps more powerful. Images of light, energy, and water are particularly appropriate to represent God's power and love. Intercessory prayer can be seen as operating like a magnifying glass that can focus and intensify God's light upon a particular point. While light is everywhere such an intensifying of light can start fires. The more persons praying, the more God's light and power can be focused upon a situation.

Another image of intercessory prayer is that of a magnet that enters and changes the magnetic fields and so attracts God's power to a particular event. A magnet refocuses energy already there. Images of opening a cloud cover, providing a prism, or tuning into sound waves for transmission, get across the same ideas about intercessory prayer. Images of water are also used. Prayer for others can be seen as an opening of flood gates or providing new channels of irrigation so a parched terrain can be watered with God's love and power. One wishes to bathe and renew another in the living waters, giving them drink and refreshment. Other ancient images are that of breath, wind, and fire. One breathes the Spirit upon a person, fans the winds of the Spirit, or fans flames of fire toward a frozen situation or an ice-cold resistant heart.

To pray for a change in another's personal intentions, or to attempt to convert the heart and mind of others, presents its own moral difficulty. Since God does not coerce, we cannot try to use the divine power in some magical way to override or overwhelm another personality. Voodoo, spells, and sorcery try to coerce others, bypassing the assent of the individual's will. And all who have loved another and seen them in the throes of self-destruction can well understand the temptation to use any means. I have many times been so desparate that a Mephistopheles or Witch of Endor could have had my soul for the price of my child's safety and salvation—a feeling Saint Paul seems to have understood. But for Christians, the freedom, conscience, and free will of the other person or persons are at stake. The self and personal conscience are sacred, for they are the ways in which human beings express their nature as made in the image of God. A self remains free either to choose good or to choose evil. How can intercessory prayer change the consciousness of another? How does one pray for the conversion or change of another's inner self?

First of all if one is praying for a person to turn to the true and good or to grow in God, then one is praying essentially for an increase in their personal freedom or liberty. Turning toward truth, goodness, and love as the divine reality, can only empower and liberate a personality. The reality principle always betters human functioning. But a person can only become more liberated by their own free act. Thus one must pray for an increase in their opportunities to hear and see God's invitations. One prays that the light will be focused more brightly and be revealed more obviously to the person in need—perhaps through chance encounters wtih others or critical experiences. One also prays that the Holy Spirit within the person may whisper more loudly. I refer to this as upping the decibel level of the Spirit's still, small voice, which is already prompting and inviting from within. The individual is free to attend or not, to harden the heart or not, but in intercessory prayer we hope to change the probabilities for paying attention.

It is important here to remember that we are told that we are members of one another, all created as the children of God imprinted with the divine image. While we may not be able to prove interconnections of human beings and human consciousness from a scientific perspective, we do believe in this union by revelation. This communal unity in the Spirit means that we are vitally connected at some deep level irrespective of differences in space or time. My prayer for you in the Spirit, with the Spirit, and through the Spirit communicates with the same Spirit within you. As a member of the human community I can add my own vicarious invitation for the increasing presence of the divine voice in your consciousness. Our elder brother Jesus always prays for you but we have also been told that a group gathered and praying in Jesus' name can help the Kingdom to come.

The whole Church formally prays for the world and all the sheep and lost lambs throughout the liturgical year. Other groups, from large religious orders to small communities, constantly engage in intercessory prayer. Groups devoted to intercessory prayer often make efforts to discern specific needs and pray for these, while at other times they pray for others in a more general way. Often one must pray that the best combination or most positive combination of events will take place, because one is not able to discern where the good lies or what evil should be avoided. At other times our prayers are more clearly focused. Some intercessory prayer groups keep logs and journals to record their prayer life and to keep track of results.

Those who pray experience the effectiveness of intercessory prayer. Persons and events are seen to be affected, often through the workings of improbable coincidences that skeptics can almost always consider "mere" coincidence. Only when the probabilities of an event become astronomically unlikely do we label it a miracle. Yet reports of miraculous cures or other miracles continue and often seem to be substantiated, although illusory correlation, the will to believe, or mass suggestion can obviously explain many accounts. Since God has once initiated a reentry into Creation in one great redemptive miracle, there is no reason other extraordinary unilateral miracles may not happen on special occasions in order to communicate symbolically. But it is well to remember that even the redemptive reentry into Creation was contingent on Mary's free assent and cooperation as a human being. Thus it more often may be the case that even in "big miracles" it is the intercessory prayer of the human faithful that makes a difference in a world given over to human stewardship and dominion. Jesus himself often pointed out the need for cooperative human faith as a necessary condition for his own works of healing.

On the other hand, lack of faith or insufficient intercessory prayer is not a ready-made reason for what may appear to be unanswered prayers. Many other explanations may apply. When prayers seem to be unanswered it may be because the specific intervention requested would not be best in the long run. Even in our own histories we can remember when we prayed fervently for something that would not have served the good of others or ourselves, although we could not see this at the time. Other situations may also arise in which the lawfulness necessary for a separate Creation, albeit one in dynamic process, has already evolved to a point where change cannot take place without disrupting the separate integrity of the created order. Death having entered into Creation, death comes to all, despite intercessory prayer. But God does appear to be the master of the contingency plan: we give God the cross, God gives us the Resurrection.

We are kept going in prayer by our experiences of directly answered prayers and by the way unexpected better solutions keep popping up when we pray about something (the contingency planner again). New doors do open and unanticipated things happen when one deals with the God of surprises. Playful surprises, too, keep us merry. No one prepares Christians to encounter the Lord of Hosts, as the master of the sporting life, full of wit, joy, parry, and ironic touches. Prayers can get answered in delicious ways, as in this small instance. A woman I know prayed to Saint Joseph for help in her large family's financial emergency. A sympathetic acquaintance heard of this and was moved to ask her husband at work to withdraw some money from their savings account and mail it anonymously. The husband sent off an arbitrarily chosen amount, leaving some money in his own account to start again, only to discover later that he had unknowingly sent the *exact* amount of the distressed family's monthly mortgage payment. "But how could anyone have known?" asked the mystified woman. Obviously, Joseph and Son are a firm that deals in little jokes, just as Teresa of Lisieux likes to scatter flowers here and there. The spiritual life is comic as well as tragic, and God acts in many ways.

PRAYING FOR THE DEAD

Why pray for the dead? If they are really dead, then we Christians are to be most pitied in having believed in the Resurrected One's promise of life after death. Perhaps there are stoic spirits who do not yearn for eternal life, but ordinary Christians do. We have hoped in the good news of an eternal life with God and our departed friends and family, a life with all suffering and injustice routed. If the good news is true then the dead are not dead but only changed; and if the dead are now with Christ and God, why do they need our prayers?

Praying for the dead can, of course, be seen as a means to reconcile ourselves to their death. Acts of intercessory prayer for our departed friends and family can do a great deal for us. Each of us must eventually come to terms with our past and in new versions of the virtue of filial piety, forgive and understand our families and early caretakers. Those persons practicing the healing of past memories through imaginative efforts to achieve reconciliation with those dead and gone, are practicing a form of praying for the dead. But does such a use of guided imagery and loving goodwill benefit the other persons as much as it does our own spiritual condition? How can the dead who are now with God need further acts of mercy and charity from us?

To pray for the dead makes us confront the mystery of the last things. While we have been told that no eye has ever seen nor mind imagined what God has prepared for us, human beings have never given up the effort. We keep seeking imaginatively to penetrate beyond the ultimate veil in order to understand our own future and to consider our present responsibilities toward the living and the dead. What of purgatory, heaven, and hell, which have played such a part in our past cultural history?

Are prayers requested for the dead because they are now in some intermediate state or purgatory in which individuals must do penance and achieve further purification or transformation before taking on the weight of glory? Most religions have believed in some form of the afterlife and religions such as Buddhism and Hinduism have been very definite in their assertion that an individual soul or self must progress through many stages and reincarnations on the way to final enlightenment. While belief in reincarnation has spread in the West, even among Christians, it remains unconvincing to those committed to the eternal reality of a separate human identity and self. How could an individual continue to be the same self while coming back in cycles of reincarnation without historical, self-conscious memory?

Memory and conscious continuity of experience through time are essential to our individual self-identity. To keep our individuality, identity, and moral responsibility, our self would have to retain conscious memories of all we have lived through. Besides, if some purifying extended journey to God is necessary there seem to be better ways this could be achieved. When viewing the breadth and density and explosive dimensions of the universe it would appear that if we must live many lives in a purgatorial way, there could be individual and group destinies other than repeated returns to this small star.

Those persons and things that we have lived with and invested in are inherently a part of our identity. Sociologists speak about reference groups and cohorts; we see how hard it is for elderly persons when the social world that was once one's own is gone. Even if, as an individual, one could be frozen and thawed in a thousand years, could one have an identity or happy life without one's own community? Thinking about how important both our individual identities and our communal social selves are, Christians imagine different versions of the last things. Dante seemed to be on the right track when he peopled the afterlife with everyone he had ever known or heard of, but he possessed a particular scientific world view and a particular version of classic culture that he integrated into his artistic and theological synthesis.

One problem with medieval images of the last things resides not so much in accepting the immortality of the individual soul, but in the fact that in our universe time and space have disappeared as eternal constants. The immortality of an individual self or soul can still make sense to us, since knowledge of DNA reveals our bodies to be basically an information program, form (soul?), or gestalt that reproduces itself by repeatedly shaping an ever-changing turnover of molecules. Even as the visible body gradually disintegrates, the programmed patterns of information and energy that make up an individual organism could well continue in a different dimension. Science fiction plays with such notions all the time. In real science we see persons who experience real pain in phantom limbs that exist experientially in built-up patterns in the brain long after the physical limb has been amputated. One can imagine a similar buildup of experiential identity and patterned information continuing after death's disintegration and dissolution of the physical body. But how all things and persons could exist simultaneously beyond time or space, or what we could experience in an afterlife, challenges our imagination.

It suddenly came to me one day that the greatest heaven that God could give any of us would be time, endless time to live the fullness of life that we enjoy right now. One hears of the mystical "eternal present," but cannot quite grasp it until facing the disappearance of one's allotment of time. Indeed, heaven could well begin here and now; it could consist of having enough time to do all of the things that one loves to do with all the people that one adores. All the way to heaven is heaven, said Teresa of Avila. Heaven could hardly be some totally alien new place apart from all the people and things that have made us what we are and that we have loved. Surely God would be more clearly manifest in heaven and the whole world would be redeemed of suffering and injustice, but heaven may be this life exploded beyond the confining limits imposed by the choices and sacrifices now necessary in time.

In this down-to-earth heaven of total fulfillment in the eternal present here and now, one could continue living and have all of the experiences that one could not have before. All of one's potentialities for creativity could be expressed and developed in cooperation with God and one's friends. One could also have all of the friends and intimates that one could not fit into this life because of family obligations or other constraints of time and place. All of the places that one wished to explore yet never could and all of the good experiences that one had to miss would finally be possible. In other words, God's incarnational heaven would be an endless time of being able to do all those things we know how to do and love to do and would like to learn to do, if we could overcome evil, our own self-limitations, and the restrictions of the external environment.

In a dark time I have also had a distinct vision of purgatory. This unwelcome insight into purgatorial suffering came to me while undergoing the most severe psychological trials of my adult experience. As I suffered a cycle of repetitive torments full of sorrow, jealousy, hate, disillusionment over betrayal, and lust for revenge, it became clear that purgatory and hell also can begin here and now just as heaven can. All the way to hell is hell. A penential purgatory could be no worse than the psychological sufferings we undergo. In a final purifying reckoning experienced outside linear time, a person could first undergo all of the suffering that he or she has caused others. It would be an appropriate form of justice if each of us were to experience the pain, torment, and trouble that our weaknesses and mean-spirited cruelties have visited upon other persons.

After such a purgation there might follow a further purification by the final experience of all of the unworthy emotions and degrading thoughts that we have wallowed in during this life. Evil thoughts torment us and keep us from the peace of Christ, as those raging in jealousy, anger, and desire for revenge know all too well. Guilt, shame, despair, and anxiety are other painful symptoms of our separation from God. It would be fitting and appropriate to experience all of the painful dross of a lifetime in one great cleansing passage to freedom and God's love and truth. How wonderful to shed all one's hatefulness and finally have the power to live in God's light and joy.

But, of course, since human beings are free, it would be theoretically possible for persons to refuse God's grace and remain in a self-chosen hell. An individual could choose isolation and elect to remain in unending suffering. When time is no more, of course, everything one chooses would be unending. Instead of shedding past suffering in order to be one with God and humanity, a person could cling to the self-torture of hate and the desire for revenge. Hell's stubborn gnawings of anger, hate, and revenge have been aptly depicted as a state of frozen despair, icy hardness of heart, and cold, proud isolation. The hellish moments we experience here and now give us a good picture of what hell is like; we need no embellishments of hellfire or demons. Our inner boredoms and despair, and the pain and nausea of no-exit torments, provide experiential previews of what human damnation might be like. Our century has already provided a plethora of examples of humanity's penchant for creating hells for the self and others.

Our intuitions about life after death stress the continuity of human experience. We have listened when Jesus says that one who sees Jesus sees God. Our experiences of human happiness and joy are the seeds of heaven just as our experiences of hell are continuous as the self and identity we create moves into the expanded dimensions beyond this world. Theologians speak of the fundamental option open to us at the moment of death, so at this critical juncture of transition we have a chance to make an even clearer, freer choice than those we have made before. The process of dying may be a birth into a newer more clearly chosen consciousness. As in the human birth process, the support of fellow human beings should be helpful. In other words, to pray for the dead is really to pray for the dying, as a support for those making the transition.

How disorienting it may be to die! The anxiety of all new and unknown journeys and endeavors must be multiplied to the millionth power. How most of us shrink from the moment, even if we are believers and expect to meet a loving and gracious Lord, and enter into a more abundant life. For those who in this life have resisted all things spiritual and all of God's promptings, it must be a traumatic shock to find oneself surviving death. Surely these persons could use the prayer and support of their fellow human beings on earth, and even more perhaps, the help of those who have already gone before. The communion of saints must take on great importance during the dying process. Christians have traditionally sought Mary's maternal aid in the childbirth they must negotiate at the moment of death. But others we have known must also be willing to help us. If in heaven we do what we love to do, surely the saints large and small who love helping others, must be ready and eager to nurture and guide their fellow human beings. Everyone could at last be a catcher in the rye, rescuing those in peril and working for the redemption of the world with all one's powers and gifts.

Christians have always had a confidence in the support and companionship of those who have gone before them in the

Lord. Stephen looked up and saw Jesus at the moment of martyrdom. It later seemed only natural to conclude that the martyrs would be ready to love and help their fellow Christians at the moment of death, as well as in the daily struggles of life. The human species has always had a lively consciousness that one's ancestors or the spirit world remain involved and concerned with their successors. As Christians we ask the saints to pray for us, just as we would ask our friends, community, parish, or prayer group for intercessory prayers. Invoking the saints, along with Mary, is a sure way an individual Christian can garner a group, or a cloud of witnesses to pray. If we love to exercise stewardship and creative nurturing efforts toward our kith and kin in the present world, why should we lose interest after death? Our cooperation with God in redeeming the world would be intensified as we became transformed and able to love the world as ardently as God does.

So in praying for the dead we are really praying for those who are dying and are being born into the human company already living and loving with God. In such a transition, there is a very fine line between praying *for* someone who is dying, and praying *to* someone who can now pray for you. Those great individuals who are on fire with the love of God before they die, have rarely been prayed "for," but instead almost instantly been prayed "to" for help. They accomplished prodigies of charity and good works in this life and obviously must be bent on continuing to do God's will in heaven. They have already been so transformed in Christ that their transition must involve an instant access of more freedom and power to do good.

Somewhere between those persons that we would immediately pray to and those persons that we would feel a real need to pray for, are those more ordinary persons who seemed on the way to adulthood in Christ's friendship but remained fairly mired in the struggle when they died. For these fundamentally good people we find ourselves praying for a certain length of time as a support and help in their dying. But we do not pray for them forever. After a while we begin to sense that we should rather be asking for their intercession. They can become one with the larger groups of persons who are prayed for collectively in the liturgical prayers of the Church. The purgatorial transition to eternity may be accomplished in a flash, but since we live in time our consciousness only gradually adjusts to our beloved dead's new status.

CONCLUSION

Intercessory prayer for others is an act of love that, like all the spiritual works of mercy, takes personal energy and effort. To pray for the living and the dead makes sense in the interdependent world revealed through God's love. But we need faith to believe in God's good news; when we flag in faith or imagination our prayers for one another also wither. Prayers of personal petition give immediate comfort and immediate results from the very process of praying, but intercessory prayer, being once removed, requires greater love of others in God, and more fidelity to the unseen. Of all the spiritual works of mercy, intercessory prayer is perhaps the most arduous because it is done with less evidence, or at least concrete evidence, to support the exertion of energy. It is always possible to doubt and consider the results of prayer to be coincidence. And in our prayers for the dead we do not even have any obvious results to turn to. Thank God the great saints have provided us with inspiring examples of perseverance in intercessory prayer. We ordinary folk are then more moved to ask the Spirit within to increase our ability to pray for the living and the dead.

EPILOGUE

Reconsidering the seven spiritual works of mercy brings to our attention the many forms of active Christian love that can exist in person-to-person encounters. Several themes have recurred in this reflective meditation. One dominant theme is the need for the Church to explore the Christian understanding of the human person in dialogue with the different disciplines of psychology. In our self-conscious era a new synthesis must be achieved if Christian spirituality is going to be effectively practiced in daily life. We have to grapple again with the basic questions, "What is human nature?" and "Is there such a thing as a Christian personality?"

In answer to the second query, I would hold that yes, certain personality characteristics will regularly appear in Christians. The spiritual works of mercy, rooted in Scripture and tradition, can only be practiced by certain kinds of persons who display certain attitudes toward other persons. Individuals who actively attempt to love others in imitation of God's love for humankind, will resemble each other in their attentiveness, patience, graciousness, kindliness, and dedication to reality. In living out their faith Christians will seek to reach out and help remedy a neighbor's ignorance, doubt, anger, bitterness, sorrow, callousness, or apathy. These personal efforts to love and care can be done in a thousand different ways, but they also display essential patterns. All those who attempt to live in Christ and with Christ, and to be a Christbearer, will begin to possess a certain family resemblance.

Another important theme emerging from these reflections is the importance of personal transformation and change. Christians are committed to constant growth in their search for perfection and fulfillment in Christ. The spiritual works of mercy are efforts to change one's self and others through specific personal transactions of love. Change comes about by individual effort and by God's initiative and freely given power. As Karl Rahner once noted, it can be hard to understand "how it is that we beg of God something that we ourselves must do." We accept through faith and love that we are in the hand of the all powerful and gracious God, and then work out our salvation in fear and trembling. We trust God, and hope for salvation, while constantly trying to change ourselves and the world. Our efforts are the sign that God is working in us.

One tries harder and harder in all kinds of ways. But the main effort we make is to open ourselves through acts of faith and love to God's power. By asking and believing that we will receive, we do receive and are slowly transformed. Our gratitude for God's gifts precedes the getting of more gifts, and these new gifts beget more gratitude and love, and so on, in endless ascending circles of giving and receiving. Those who have, get more; the grateful in gratitude give more, and end up getting even more. The spiritual economy of the Trinity is based on infinite plenitude and what the mystics have called "God's fecund nature." As Blesed Jan van Ruysbroeck says, "And this work is ever new; beginning, operating, and being fulfilled; and herein we are blessed in knowing, loving, and being fulfilled together with God."*

---

*The Seven Steps of the Ladder of Spiritual Love (London: Dacre Press, A. & C. Black, 1952), p. 61.

The Spirit within moves us to love and open up to other persons in need. As we try to reach out we are ourselves transformed. Over and over we see that the relationship of self to other is dependent upon our inner relationship of self to self, which is in turn dependent on the self's relationship to God. There are three elements in this interacting system which cannot be separated. To minister to your need, I must acknowledge both my own need and my own help from God and my fellows. To comfort you I must have suffered, been comforted, and be comfortable. To instruct your ignorance I must be in touch with my own ignorance, my present knowing, and the movements needed to obtain enlightenment. And it is the same with our personal confrontations with human doubt, anger, bitterness, and apathy. Knowing one's self, finding one's self, and expending one's self for another are intertwined activities. Love of self, love of God, and love of neighbor are interdependent.

Gradually and painfully we become psychologically integrated and whole as we grow up into Christ. As we become healed we can heal. In the beginning we may only be able to ask for an increase of desire. Never mind the difficulties involved in doing good, just help me to *want* to be good. The ancient religious cry of the heart is perpetually renewed, "O Lord, give me a transformed living loving heart instead of this hard heart of stone." It is probably true that with God's grace we can be as holy as we want to be, but wanting to be holy is the crux of the matter. Much of our prayer life and worship is devoted to attentively kindling the flame of love and desire, which then makes all effort seem effortless.

A final theme emerges from meditating on the spiritual works of mercy. While the corporal works of mercy are basically aimed at the restoration of health, the spiritual works of mercy are aimed at making human beings happy. Happiness and joy are the marks of the Spirit. Christ came to give us joy and happiness, even though this Gospel message always seems too good to be true. The reason Christians must work to overcome sin, ignorance, doubt, sorrow, anger, bitterness, and despair is that God wants us to be happy and live fully and abundantly. Only as we grow together in love will we be able to leave the sadness, gloom, and anxiety of sin behind. We are drawn by the Spirit to the warming fire of joy, and the lure of the divine work to be done. God works through us to perform the spiritual works of mercy. With each person's transformation achieved, "Amazing Grace shall then prevail, in heaven's joy and peace."